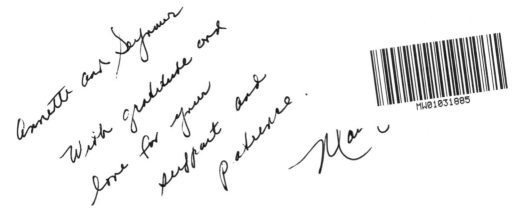

Annette and Seymour
With gratitude and
love for your
support and
patience.
Mar

Inquiring into Teaching and Learning

Explorations & Discoveries for Prospective Teachers

Second Edition

Marilyn Sobelman
New York University

Maris H. Krasnow
New York University

KENDALL/HUNT PUBLISHING COMPANY
4050 Westmark Drive   Dubuque, Iowa 52002

D E D I C A T I O N

The inspiration, support, and constant guidance that Mark Alter generously provided throughout the years that he served as Chair of the Department of Teaching and Learning strengthened us as educators, writers, and thinkers. He has been, and always will be, our dearest colleague, mentor, and friend. We are deeply indebted to him for encouraging us to write *Inquiring into Teaching and Learning,* a text that represents our department's core offering.

Our goal is to invite prospective teachers to explore the purposes and processes of teaching and learning. Most important, we strive to help our readers appreciate and respect the vibrant diversity among the schools and children of our city, the schools and children to which Mark has devoted his heart, mind, and energy.

We dedicate this second edition to Mark Alter with our thanks and love.

CONTENTS

REMEMBERING 9/11

September 11, 2001. As this text goes to press, New York City, our city, has just experienced a terrorist attack on the World Trade Center, the worst, most unimaginable catastrophe. We are both New Yorkers who teach at New York University in the heart of this city. We have long since dedicated our efforts to advancing the growth of teaching and learning, working with teachers and prospective teachers, in and out of their classrooms. As teacher educators, we commit ourselves anew to supporting them as they face the overwhelming challenge of helping themselves and their students deal with the emotional and physical trauma of these awful days. Theirs is a heavy burden, an awesome responsibility. They must struggle to understand the forces surrounding this tragedy and nurture students and colleagues who have suffered devastating losses within their families and circles of friends. At the same time they must develop the ability, the energy, and the resolve to help themselves and their students participate in the rebuilding and strengthening of our communities and our country. We stand with them and look with hope to the future.

M. S.
M. H. K.

FOREWORD

At a time when many teachers and teacher educators are under attack for presumed incompetence, Marilyn Sobelman and Maris Krasnow have developed a text that demonstrates the opposite. It is thoughtful, inspiring, and provides a powerful vision of the nature of teaching, learning, and teacher education that shows both how complex these processes are and how well competent professionals are working to improve all aspects of schooling.

Teachers and teacher educators are under attack by people outside of education who presume to know that schools are failing and that the blame for such failure can be laid squarely on the teachers and those who have miseducated them. Even people of goodwill who are sincerely concerned with improving schools are convinced that the schooling problems they see (or have heard about) are soluble with a few simple changes: more tests, higher standards, and more subject content. They believe that the tests will hold students, teachers, and administrators accountable, that setting standards will fully define what all children should know and be able to do, and that focusing on content and not teaching methods will ensure that the school curriculum and the academic background of the teachers will be filled with appropriate knowledge. Like many political solutions to complex social problems, these "solutions" in practice turn out to be reductive, distorting, and, in some ways, they exacerbate rather than solve whatever the original problem really was.

This is not the place for a full analysis of all of these issues, but instead to praise this text as one that clearly reveals the inadequacy of such "solutions" by showing a richer and more effective path to school reform: *the effective preparation of teachers who will be prepared to serve as highly competent professionals.* No one denies the need for school accountability, but too many tests limit rather than enrich the schooling experience. No one is in favor of low standards, but reducing the determination of how they are being achieved to test scores alone effectively eliminates all of those standards that we cannot easily and mechanically test. And most of all, no one denies the importance of teacher knowledge as a basis for promoting student knowledge acquisition, but unless teachers know how to help *all* children learn, their expert subject matter knowledge will be insufficient as a basis for effective teaching. What this book and the program it grew from promotes are teachers with pedagogical content knowledge who integrate their subject matter expertise with insights into teaching and learning and students and teachers in the context of schools.

Teacher education begins with helping prospective and new teachers make the transition from student to teacher. Though this may seem easy and automatic enough, in practice it isn't. The thousands of hours we spend as students teach us a lot about schools and teaching, but like the Wizard of Oz, until we are making that transition we have no idea what goes on behind the curtain. We also quite naturally tend to believe that our experience in school constitutes the norm and that others learn as we do. So when we come to teacher education, we have already developed a set of implicit beliefs and tacit theories about teaching and learning that will determine how we teach unless they are challenged. Since research has shown overwhelmingly that teachers teach as they were taught unless that cycle is interrupted, this book, and the program of study it initiates, challenges those beliefs and theories with the goal of helping teachers make deliberate choices about how and what to teach.

By starting with their own learning autobiography and the autobiographies of other learners and teachers, prospective and beginning teachers are asked to see how their learning experiences in and out of school have determined their current stance. They are asked, in effect, are your current beliefs and theories those you want to start with or are you open to change? Sharing these beliefs and experiences with their peers also provides a way of seeing more diversity among learners and provides the first step toward reexamining these tacit theories. Next comes reading and writing about how people learn, about the roles of language, race, class, and gender in learning, and about how individual learning patterns enhance or inhibit achievement. The goal is not to force change on future teachers, but to ensure that if they teach as they were taught they will do so on the basis of a well-thought-out choice after considering several alternatives. We don't want to throw the baby out with the bathwater, but first we must learn how to tell the difference between the two.

Unlike most texts that only demand engagement and absorption, this one requires active transactions as readers interrogate the issues it raises and their own learning histories. There is information here aplenty, but it will only come alive as it becomes transformed into insights and actions that can have impact on the teaching/learning experiences of the reader's classroom. Teacher education students are not expected to simply amass facts and theories or even plans and activities unless they will be applicable to their professional practice. So the proof of this book, course, and program will come when it is enacted. And even if there is a long gap between reading and action, if the book does its job, the reader will be sufficiently changed by the experience of enacting the learning processes invited by this text, and the cycle of teaching as we were taught will finally be broken.

No teacher education program completely prepares teachers for the real world of the classrooms they will teach in. Just as medical students require three to seven years of clinical experience before they are fully competent practitioners, so too teachers need to develop their clinical skills both during their teacher education curricula and during their first three to five years of teaching. This text provides the basis for the processes of clinical learning essential to making the transition from student to novice to expert by pairing a vision of an ideal pedagogy with an understanding of the context of the constraints of the real world of schools where pedagogy is actually lived. Maris Krasnow and Marilyn Sobelman are committed to educating teachers who will have a complex vision of teaching and learning that they will use as the basis of their own professional growth and as an agent of change in the schools they work in.

But we all backslide now and then. The power of our individual and collective commonsense experiences runs deep. They determine what we believe are the norms of schooling, and we continually fall back on such normative practices. The only sure way to struggle against such backsliding and to keep up the struggle toward what I call uncommon sense (Mayher, 1990) is through reflection and change. Effective teachers know that teaching is too complex to ever be done perfectly. Even after 5 or 10 or 20 years of experience there will be new challenges to face and new problems to solve. So the only way to keep on improving is to research our own practice, to reflect on what went well and what was difficult, and to make plans to change tomorrow and next week on the basis of what we learned today.

The overall goal of the NYU teacher education program is the preparation of beginning and experienced teachers who will be such reflective practitioners. And that preparation process begins with and is enacted in this book. Prospective and beginning teachers who engage with its pages will be the teachers we need for America's future.

John S. Mayher
New York University
August 2005

PREFACE

This second edition of *Inquiring into Teaching and Learning* extends the boundaries of the original book, although the primary purpose remains the same: to provide the frameworks to support prospective teacher-learners setting off on their professional studies. Through these explorations we hope to encourage future teachers to identify and pursue the complex and multidimensional nature of teaching and learning. This book should not be perceived as a text on methods or curriculum development, but should serve as a guide to help you identify the criteria for good teaching and learning experiences.

As was true of our first endeavor, this new version builds upon the course on which it was based, New York University's "Inquiries into Teaching and Learning." In 1993, after three years of intensive collaborative planning, the faculty of the Department of Teaching and Learning at New York University's Steinhardt School of Education introduced a two-semester sequence entitled "Inquiries into Teaching and Learning: Uncovering What Is; Imagining What Might Be." "Inquiries," as it quickly became known, was designed to frame the Department's undergraduate and graduate preservice teacher education programs and establish a foundation for the students' subsequent studies, regardless of their chosen grade level or content field. Among the curriculum planners were the authors of this text: Marilyn Sobelman, who became the course coordinator, and Maris H. Krasnow, who piloted the course and has continued to teach it.

The Inquiries curriculum development process closely resembled what weavers do as they create their richly patterned, loosely designed cloth. The warp, the strong threads running lengthwise on the loom, is represented by four themes: learners and learning, knowledge and knowing, teachers and teaching, schools and schooling. The woof or horizontal yarns are the four strands, the threads that produce the hues and nubs of the fabric's texture: autobiography, diversity, collaboration, reflection. The course design, as well as the design for this text, results from the interlacing of the four strands across the four themes. And, as in the case of artisan weavers, the course and the way the text can be used varies, shaped by the talents and interests of individual teachers, the learning histories, interests, and cultures of the readers, and the changing issues and directions in the educational world and society at large.

Over the years, the roller coaster of politics and the emergence of new research and new knowledge caused us to modify Inquiries to be consistent with our commitment to keep it fresh, focused, and current. Despite these revisions, the essential elements of the original conception remain constant.

We have benefited greatly from the feedback of students and instructors who employed our first edition in their teacher education classes. As a response to their experiences, for this second edition we have added new chapters to expand the dimensions of teaching and learning. We identify a range of rapidly changing innovations and dilemmas that new teachers are likely to meet as they enter the field, raise several additional issues, and invite our readers' attention to controversial approaches confronting the profession.

Throughout the text we highlight the theories and discoveries of many researchers, scholars, and practitioners and urge you to obtain the full texts of these writers whose contributions we can only mention briefly. In addition, in each chapter we have posed questions in italics and offered suggestions for the kinds of explorations that you might undertake either independently or with colleagues.

For many readers this text may seem unusual because our pedagogy and discussions challenge the way information is usually transmitted from teacher to student. In the past, you may have succeeded in school by following rules, memorizing information, and passing tests. Although we are both products of such schooling, our classroom experiences as teachers led us to pursue and study more meaningful ways of knowing. Here we challenge you to examine new ways of learning and teaching and new strategies to develop and articulate your own growing ideas and beliefs.

Some readers find our educational practice uncomfortable, difficult, and risky and resist the challenge. Others find it liberating, eagerly take the risks, and slowly develop their confidence as they explore the unknown. We will do our best to help you understand and struggle with your doubts, and support you as you break through your discomfort with some of the ideas presented. For your part, we ask that you play both the "believing" game and the "doubting" game (Elbow, 1973). In other words, we urge you to see the world from other vantage points and imagine why they might be valid. At the same time, you should question your own and others' ideas as you search for deeper understandings. We cannot require you to change your mind, but we ask you to consider critically both your beliefs and ours as you begin to formulate an informed educational philosophy.

We bring to the authoring of this text our accumulated experiences of collaborating with our colleagues over a period of 15 years. We worked with hundreds of instructors in implementing the Inquiries courses, and we listened to thousands of students who shared their Inquiries stories with us. We observed and taught classes, read students' portfolios, participated in meetings with instructors, and analyzed course evaluations. Therefore, what we propose has been "field tested" and reflects what we have learned and want to share with you. We have listed our e-mail addresses in the hope that you will communicate with us and let us know how you are progressing. We look forward to receiving your reactions, questions, and suggestions so that we can learn from you.

As teachers, we are constantly discovering new ways to rejuvenate our thinking and our practice. We hope that *Inquiring into Teaching and Learning* will be an enlightening experience for you.

Marilyn Sobelman   Maris H.Krasnow
mes1@nyu.edu   mk29@nyu.edu

ACKNOWLEDGMENTS

Collaboration remains the cornerstone of our work. By sharing and learning from each other we believe we were better able to see the needed elaborations that led to this second edition. In addition to the collaboration we have enjoyed, we owe our deep appreciation to many individuals who, knowingly and unknowingly, collaborated with us in our endeavor:

To our colleagues in the Department of Teaching and Learning at NYU's Steinhardt School of Education who inspired us by example and offered us suggestions based on their experiences using our first edition. They number too many to be listed here, but we hope they know that our efforts reflect their wisdom and their support.

To Dr. James W. Fraser, a noted historian of education and visiting professor, whose interest in our model and engagement with our course supported our evolving work. How fortunate we were that he was here during the 2004–2005 academic year.

To all the Inquiries instructors with whom we worked over time. As they devoted their energies to teaching the Inquiries courses, their unique perspectives prodded our thinking and enriched our writing. We benefited especially from the feedback we received from Dr. Mary Leou, Tracy Daraviras, Boyce Durr, and Cynthia Shor who piloted our two new chapters. Their enthusiasm and commitment encouraged us to improve upon our initial work.

To our preservice teacher education students—undergraduate and graduate—who often challenged us and sometimes resisted us, but taught us as much or more than we taught them.

To Raina Krasnow for her graphics expertise and Tony Chen for his technical assistance.

From Marilyn: To my families, the East Coast Sobelmans and the West Coast Sobelman-Sterns, for sustaining me with pride and purpose.

From Maris: To my husband, Jesse, and daughters, Freya, Fallyn, and Raina, for their inspiration, patience, and unconditional love.

We include among our roles daughter, sister, wife, mother, grandmother, student, teacher, colleague, and friend. In each role, we are strengthened by the people around us and by those whose memories we cherish. Our indebtedness to them is beyond measure.

CHAPTER 1

Setting the Stage

Preparing Teachers for the 21st Century

Education is a profession embroiled in never-ending controversies, increasingly rating front-page headlines in newspapers across the country. Toward the end of the 20th century and at the onset of the 21st century, the educational debates have become more highly publicized and polarized than ever before. The roots of the current rhetoric were probably planted by the 1983 publication of *A Nation at Risk* (1984), the report of the National Commission on Excellence in Education. That report claimed that our schools were suffering from a "rising tide of mediocrity," and that the declining level of student performance threatened our country's international relations and economic security. Since then, critics and advocates from the left, the right, and the middle of the educational and political spectrums have been taking strong positions about "the crisis" in our schools. They attribute the problems to a whole range of factors, from the use of the "wrong" methodologies to underallocated financial resources to shifts in student demographics.

Educational historians have documented cyclical shifts during which more, or less, attention has been paid to such educational issues as standardized testing and evaluation, immigration and population trends, national identity, and "back to basics." In times of economic stress, schools are one of the first social institutions deeply affected; students, families, and educational personnel engaged in the creative arts, extracurricular activities, support services, special programs, and libraries suffer the most. Clearly, it is those in power who swing the pendulum, separating society's winners from its losers. Through it all, teachers have learned to accommodate to constant change, some of which has proved valuable. Yet, when there is widespread dissatisfaction with some forms of student achievement, teachers regularly become the scapegoats for criticism and increased attention is directed toward their preparation.

One of the most dramatic responses to the public outcry appeared in 1996, the result of an intensive 2-year study by the National Commission on Teaching and America's Future. In *What Matters Most: Teaching for America's Future* (1996), the Commission claims that an "investment in teaching" is a "missing link" in achieving the needed reforms.

> *Rather than proclamations, schools need policies and working environments that attract the best people to teaching, provide them superb preparation, hone their skills and commitment in the early years, and keep them in the profession by rewarding them for their knowledge, skills and good work. (p. 5)*

The subsequent clamor from varied sectors of the population has prompted many states in the United States to institute grade-level standards for students and to revise their teacher certification requirements to include more liberal arts and content specialization, more pedagogical rigor, more attention to special education, and more field-based experiences. In addition to each individual state's revised requirements, standards have emerged from the various professional associations—for early childhood teachers, English language arts teachers, teachers of mathematics, teachers of social studies, teachers of science, and so forth. In almost every instance, we find that new learning standards for students have been accompanied by new standards for teachers.

At about the same time that these initiatives were being taken, the influential National Board for Professional Teaching Standards, seeking to identify and recognize outstanding teachers, formulated five "core propositions" as the basis for awarding national board certification (http://www.nbpts.org/about/coreprops.cfm). They pronounced that teachers should:

Be committed to students and their learning.

Know the subjects they teach and how to teach those subjects to students.

Be responsible for managing and monitoring student learning.

Think systematically about their practice and learn from experience.

Be members of learning communities.

These propositions, though hardly new, established nationwide expectations. Geared for experienced teachers, the National Board's criteria support the notion that teacher expertise is developed over time.

Although we believe that preservice teacher preparation is just the first formal phase in a teacher's ongoing journey, we acknowledge that even at this stage, the educational climate of the 21st century exacts high demands. The novice's route is likely to be bumpy, with detours, hindrances, and surprises, but motivated and caring prospective teachers, given support and encouragement, will overcome the obstacles.

We concede that teacher preparation is no guarantee for success, but there's a good chance that when it is characterized by a sincere commitment to enacting an integrated set of beliefs and practices, a confident and competent beginner will emerge. In *Inquiring into Teaching and Learning* we suggest how the initial exploration could progress.

> *Can you identify ways in which your own educational experiences reflected the conditions of teaching and learning at that time? What do you see today as the major strengths, problems, and controversies in the field of education?*

Rationale for a Prospective Teacher's Inquiry

The conceptual framework for this text is based on the integration of theories and pedagogical principles drawn from various disciplines. Many of these powerful ideas are succinctly expressed in John Mayher's *Uncommon Sense* (1990), where he offers a vision of teacher education:

> If this book has a single theme, it is that schools must be dramatically changed if they are to fulfill their educational mission in a democratic society. Teachers are the only people who have the power, the commitment, the desire, and the capacity to be leaders in the process of change. But to take on such leadership roles we must substantially change our conceptions of the nature and processes of schooling. Doing so will not be easy, since most of these conceptions have not been the subject of professional scrutiny and analysis. Questioning such assumptions requires both examining and reinterpreting the meaning of our learning experiences in and out of school by looking at them through new theoretical lenses. (p. 1)

Mayher challenges teacher educators to ask:

> *What do we believe about teaching and learning? How might learners learn most effectively? What are the critical ideas and issues prospective teachers should explore?*

In response to these questions, we present a brief explanation of our beliefs, and suggest how each one is related to the others to form a composite foundation for our approach to the study of teaching and learning. In later chapters, we expand on these ideas and show how they impact upon the conduct of your inquiries.

Social Constructivism

Perhaps the most fundamental and enduring belief we hold is that knowledge is socially constructed, that people make sense of the world by reconstruing their individual experiences and understandings in ongoing dialogues where they learn with and from others. Social constructivism, itself an amalgam relying on the work of John Dewey (1938), Jean Piaget (Piaget & Inhelder, 1969), and Lev Vygotsky (1978), has been expanded and given instructional application by cognitive psychologists. Catherine Twomey Fosnot (1996) defines constructivism as a "theory . . . that construes learning as an interpretive, recursive, building process by active learners interacting with the physical and social world" (p. 20). When applying constructivism to teacher education, Fosnot maintains that teachers "need to be engaged in learning experiences that confront traditional beliefs, in experiences where they can study children and their meaning-making, and in field experiences where they can experiment collaboratively" (p. 216).

Lauren Resnick (1991) uses the term *shared cognition* to characterize the interaction between social and cognitive processes. She maintains that "much of human cognition is so varied and so sensitive to cultural contexts that we must also seek mechanisms by which people actively shape each other's knowledge and reasoning processes" (p. 2). Moreover, Resnick argues that we need to recognize "the idea of knowledge as distributed across several individuals whose interactions determine decisions, judgments, and problem solutions" (p. 3).

According to Brooks and Brooks (1999), five overarching principles should be evident in constructivist classrooms (p. ix):

1. Teachers seeking and valuing their students' points of view.
2. Classroom activities challenging students' suppositions.
3. Teachers posing problems of emerging relevance.
4. Teachers building lessons around primary concepts and "big" ideas.
5. Teachers assessing student understanding in the context of daily teaching.

In a socially constructivist classroom, students, their peers, and instructors are engaged in uncovering their own meanings. When they examine those ideas together, learning multiplies for all participants.

Exploratory Talk and Writing

Consistent with social constructivism is our belief that exploratory talk in small groups and exploratory writing enable individuals to uncover meanings. Through such processes, learners "make connections, re-arrange, re-conceptualize, and internalize the new experiences, ideas, and ways of knowing offered in the curriculum" (Barnes, 1992, p. 6). In an essay that profoundly influenced many teachers, James Britton (1982) hypothesizes that we "may be underestimating the importance of 'shaping at the point of utterance.' " He says:

When we start to speak, we push the boat out and trust it will come to shore somewhere—not anywhere, which would be tantamount to losing our way, but somewhere that constitutes a stage on a purposeful journey. To embark on a conversational utterance is to take on a certain responsibility, to stake a claim that calls for justification; and perhaps it is the social pressure on the speaker to justify his claim that gives talk an edge over silent brooding as a problem-solving procedure. (p. 139)

As students talk and write to learn, discussing and exploring their writings, class readings, and personal ideas with their peers, a wide range of perspectives and possibilities comes forth to inform everyone's understanding and decision-making processes. Today's technology, offering email, web boards, chat rooms, and instant messaging, further enhances the opportunities to deepen one's explorations on one's own, while online communication allows the dialogue to continue with others at all times.

Autobiography

A third belief is that new learning is built out of the reconstruction of past experience and personal history. Autobiography, the narrative recounting of critical moments in one's life, encourages an examination of how one arrives at assumptions about self and society and leads to the reframing of beliefs and practices. Jerome Bruner (1990) contends that narrative provides an important form of knowledge and if shared, through guided self-reflection, can increase one's insight and perspective even further. William Pinar (1998) claims that autobiography helps people examine and transform themselves while gaining insights into others.

Describing autobiography as a map-making journey, Patrick Diamond (1995) writes:

By learning to become scholars of our own experience and consciousness, following the navigation lights of our own construction processes, we can begin our educational journey. When we position self, and not powerful others, at the center of the cosmology that we project onto life, we can reconsider the known constellations of ideas and practices. The chief resource that we each bring to this work is us, the persons we are, the viewpoints that we represent, and the concerns that we voice. We mark our way through the universe by our inquiries. These enable us to reflect on all our undertakings. (p. 80)

Prospective teachers are influenced by their personal histories and formulate their ideas according to these experiences (Britzman, 1986; Bullough, 1989, 1990; Kagan, 1992; Schubert, 1990). Both positive and negative teacher role models can influence their selection of teaching as a profession, as does family tradition for some. The familiarity factor (Feiman-Nemser & Buchman, 1983) also promotes this choice. "Teachers and potential teachers were all once students and many hold deeply to the image of teachers and teaching they remember" (Krasnow, 1993, p. 3). Through the uncovering of their learning autobiographies, prospective teachers can become aware of the various dynamics that influenced their growth and development.

Deborah P. Britzman (1991) raises the bar by claiming that engaging students of education in autobiographical study can lead them to critically examining their assumptions and reshaping their beliefs and behaviors.

In the case of student teachers, understanding the contradictory dynamics of their own biography can empower them to determine the interventions necessary to move beyond the sway of cultural authority. The concern should be with how we become entangled in and can become disentangled from the dynamics of cultural reproduction. And because education is always about interventions and the struggles of authorization—in the realm of the cognitive, the affective, the social, and the cultural—it behooves those learning to teach to rethink how social forces and dominant categories of meaning intervene in and organize their own lives and the lives of their students. (p. 233)

Diversity

We believe that recognizing differences of viewpoint and differences of culture is essential to understanding oneself, one's colleagues, one's students, and one's society. Jerome Bruner (1990) reminds us that such awareness begins with the teacher's open-mindedness, which he defines as "a willingness to construe knowledge and values from multiple perspectives without loss of commitment to one's own." This, he says, is "the keystone of what we call a democratic culture" (p. 30). Of course, one may find occasions where one needs to change one's commitment or change one's mind.

Lisa Delpit (1995) writes:

We can continue to view diversity as a problem, attempting to force all differences into standardized boxes. Or we can recognize that diversity of thought, language, and worldview in our classrooms cannot only provide an exciting educational setting, but can also prepare our children for the richness of living in an increasingly diverse national community. (p. 66)

Through constructive discourse about different identities, including race, religion, class, language, age, gender, sexual orientation, ability, and disability, future teachers learn to recognize and appreciate the range of factors that contributes to how people think and feel, learn and act, in and out of school. At the same time, they come to terms with their own beliefs, perceptions, attitudes, and autobiographical history.

Reflection

A fifth tenet is that reflective practice strengthens professionals by inviting them to see their work as problematic. Donald Schön (1983), building on Dewey, explains: "It is . . . through the non-technical process of framing the problematic situation that we may organize and clarify both the ends to be achieved and the possible means of achieving them" (p. 41). We support Schön's claim that reflection "leads us to recognize that the scope of technical expertise is limited by situations of uncertainty, instability, uniqueness, and conflict" (p. 345). In assuming this stance, we are affirmed by Linda Darling-Hammond and Velma Cobb (1996) who note that "teacher preparation and teacher induction programs are increasingly introducing strategies that help teachers develop a reflective and problem-solving orientation." This is achieved, they report, "by engaging [teachers] in teacher research, in school-based inquiry, and in learning about students' experiences so that they are building an empirical understanding of learners and a capacity to analyze and reflect on their practice" (p. 43).

In their introductory text devoted to reflective teaching, teacher educators Kenneth M. Zeichner and Daniel P. Liston (1996) explain:

> . . . it is through reflection on our teaching that we become more skilled, more capable, and in general better teacher . . . although some types of reflection have us focused more on the content that we teach, others tend to highlight either our students and their learning, or the contexts in which we teach . . . despite these different conceptions of reflective teaching, they all share an emphasis on examining the thoughts and understandings that we bring to our teaching and the efforts in which we are engaged while we are teaching. (p. xvii)

We contend that reflective practice promotes the development of teachers who think deeply and critically about the relationships among their work, themselves, their students, the curriculum, and the world. When teachers model reflective inquiry they are inviting their students to reflect with them about the ongoing events of their classroom and communities. As students take on the reflective stance, they apply it to their own understandings as learners and citizens.

Negotiation

Learning to negotiate begins early in life—between mothers and infants, and among toddlers in the sandbox. The child who relinquishes the shovel, indicating a willingness to share, has respected or satisfied another child's need while gaining personal satisfaction as well. As is true in this illustration, negotiation reaps benefits for all the parties involved. As we mature, successful negotiation requires the refinement of skills and strategies such as listening, articulating a viewpoint, understanding others' points of view, reading verbal and nonverbal patterns of communication, and maintaining an attitude of mutual respect. Learning the art of negotiation facilitates the building of all kinds of relationships, both personal and professional.

In the educational world, negotiation occurs at all points on the organizational continuum. Teachers may negotiate with administrators, colleagues, and parents, but the key aspects of negotiation take place in the classroom. Although curriculum preplanning is needed, we hold firmly to the notion that curriculum is always tentative and fluid, to be negotiated among teachers, among students, and between teachers and students.

> Negotiating the curriculum means deliberately planning to invite students [and teachers] to contribute to, and to modify, the educational program, so that they will have a real investment both in the learning journey and in the outcome. (Boomer, 1992, p. 14)

Negotiation among teachers and students has the added value of safeguarding the curriculum from both bias and stagnation. Through negotiation, new ideas, new findings, and new approaches can be heard, assessed, modified, and integrated. Negotiation, however, is not problem-free. Tensions may arise during decision making, but the act of hearing everyone's perspective ensures that the voices of all members of the group are respected, treated fairly, and that their participation is valued.

We recognize that negotiation is a learned skill, one that needs to be integrated into teacher education programs. It is a delicate process requiring teachers to be flexible as they think on their feet and listen to their students and their colleagues. It requires teachers to sustain their overall goals, yet be prepared to relinquish their preferred sequence, activity, or instructional mode.

Collaboration

Despite a full and busy workday and a classroom filled with students, a teacher's day may be lonely and isolated. Meaningful opportunities for teachers to commune with peers or other adults in the school day are rare (Sarason, 1971, p. 106). According to Madeline Grumet (1989), ". . . the isolation of teachers from each other and from the parents of their students has weakened teachers' abilities to influence the curriculum, the culture of the school, and the remuneration and working conditions of their shared enterprise" (p. 15). Collaboration extends beyond the classroom to include the home, the meeting room, and the boardroom. It strengthens parent–teacher relationships and school–community alliances. We believe it is critical to reduce the insularity of teachers and to ensure that collaboration becomes a vital part of the teacher's practice.

Just as people need to learn to negotiate they must also learn to collaborate. A climate of trust should prevail and all voices including the negative must be heard (Fullan, 1993). It is pivotal that teachers work as partners, not working at cross-purposes but finding common ground. To reach a common goal or to arrive at consensus, participants must be prepared to try many paths, identify and reconcile disparate positions, and refine, modify, and expand their individual understandings.

Teachers who value collaboration also see it as a necessary component of a positive classroom environment. They enable their students to succeed in many different situations by providing collaborative activities and assignments that enrich the learning process.

Active Learning

An old Chinese proverb says:

I hear and I forget;
I see and I remember;
I do and I understand.

For the most part, students have spent their lives in passive teaching and learning roles and environments. Teachers are experts delivering information and students are memorizers, expected to save and eventually feed it all back. Paolo Freire (1970) refers to this model as the banking method of education.

As the Chinese proverb suggests, we believe that learning is internalized when learners are actively engaged. John Dewey (1929) maintains, "there is no such thing as genuine knowledge and fruitful understanding except as the offspring of doing" (p. 321). For students to develop new understanding and to learn they must be directly involved in the processes of inquiring, experimenting, creating, discovering, sharing, and applying. Examples of active learning may include collaborative learning, problem-based learning, case methods, projects, simulations, and interactive technology.

The visual and performing arts further widen opportunities for active learning. Singing, dancing, drawing, and acting offer new lenses from which students can explore the world. Not only do they learn new content, they also begin to see the ways in which the arts connect to their everyday lives and can be used as a powerful means of expression and communication. Developing the structures and routines that go into a craft later on may contribute to a student's growth and development in other areas. Most important, regularly engaging students in the arts helps to identify their special talents that may go unnoticed. Engaging in play provides young children with active learning. Here, too, children create their own experiences as they interact with their peers and teachers.

We should, however, heed Dewey's (1929) warning: "Mere activity does not constitute experience." Thoughtful interaction must include opportunities for students and teachers to deconstruct the events that lead to learning. These engagements must result in the learner's ongoing growth. Then, as Dewey emphasizes, "When an activity is continued into the undergoing consequences, when the change made by action is reflected back into a change made in us, the mere flux is loaded with significance. We learn something" (p. 163).

Teachers need to develop a variety of teaching and learning strategies that strengthen their students' mastery of concepts, skills, and abilities, enabling them to become self-directed, productive, and fulfilled learners. Both teachers and students should see learning as personally meaningful, collaborative, dynamic, and enjoyable.

Democracy

We heartily endorse the thesis that "the school is peculiarly the institution in which democracy becomes conscious of itself" (Bode, 1950, p. 95). We want classrooms to be places where students go, "not merely to learn, but to carry on a way of life" (p. 77), where there is a "proper account of individual differences and . . . reliance on the principle of community living" (p. 82).

Dewey (1929) also writes about education as a social process and describes society as needing "a type of education which gives individuals a personal interest in social relationships and control, and the habits of mind which secure social changes without introducing disorder" (p. 115).

For Michael Apple and James Beane (1995), seven principles are implicit in democratic schools:

1. The open flow of ideas, regardless of their popularity, that enables people to be as fully informed as possible.
2. Faith in the individual and the collective capacity of people to create possibilities for resolving problems.
3. The use of critical reflection and analysis to evaluate ideas, problems, and policies.
4. Concern for the welfare of others and the "common good."
5. Concern for the dignity and rights of individuals and minorities.
6. An understanding that democracy is not so much an *ideal* to be pursued as an *idealized* set of values that we must live and that must guide our lives as a people.
7. The organization of social institutions to promote and extend the democratic way of life. (pp. 6–7)

In microcosm, each classroom should reflect the goals of the school and take its mission seriously. Gordon Pradl's study (1996) of literature as a social act underscores what is essential to a democratic classroom:

Acknowledging the rightful claim of each reader's uniqueness begins the practice of democracy, which then includes sharing responses across persons and tentatively exploring mutual understandings—shifting between what separates and what ties together. (p. 149)

Teachers are leading players in bringing the principles of democracy to the forefront of the classroom. Together with their students they must learn to use these tools to create an environment where democratic living leads to learning and democratic learning leads to living.

Themes and Strands

The structure of our text integrates the nine principles just mentioned to form our conceptual framework into four themes and four strands. Figure 1.1 shows the themes and strands and their interwoven relationships. We have created questions, Figure 1.2, for each theme for you to contemplate. The creation of this framework draws upon knowledge and research from many disciplines, including educational history and philosophy, psychology, sociology, linguistics, and literary theory.

What thoughts come to mind as you study these figures? What questions interest you? What questions surprise you? What questions would you add? We hope your engagement with this text will lead you to many new explorations and discoveries.

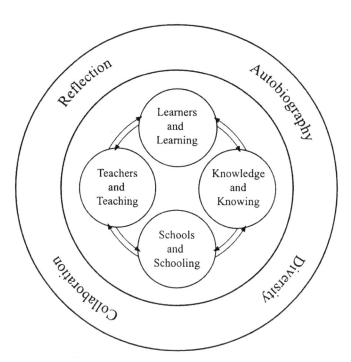

Figure 1.1 Inquiries into Teaching and Learning, Themes and Strands

Strands	Theme 1: Learners and Learning	Theme 2: Knowledge and Knowing
Autobiography Diversity Collaboration Reflection	• How do people learn? • Do all people learn the same way? • How do we know learning has occurred? • How do we asses learning? • Who is the *we* in this question? • What is the relationship between learning and teaching?	• How is knowledge defined and constructed in different cultures? • What is worth knowing? • How is that decided and by whom? • What is the link between knowledge and action? • What do teachers need to know? • How is knowledge assessed?

Strands	Theme 3: Teachers and Teaching	Theme 4: Schools and Schooling
Autobiography Diversity Collaboration Reflection	• What does it mean to teach? • Who is teaching for? • What is a teacher's responsibility to self, to others, to school, to community? • What are the relationships between teaching a subject and teaching students? • What values and strategies must teachers possess to transform schools?	• What are schools for? • What do schools value? • Whose values do schools represent? • How do schools relate to their communities? • What are the power relationships among people in schools? • If schools are not what they might be, how can they be changed?

Figure 1.2 Inquiries into Teaching and Learning: The Questions

Learners and Learning

Creating a learning community requires attention to a range of intricate variables, including the learning process, the teaching process, the characteristics of a group's members, and the purposes for which the group has assembled. To complicate matters further, there is neither a single acceptable theory of learning nor a single agreed-upon approach to teaching. There is neither an approved list of student characteristics nor a set of common objectives applicable to all learners.

In Chapter 1, we set forth the principles and approaches that guide our thinking and our practice. We value the theory of social constructivism because it integrates individual and collaborative learning. It recognizes that learners have their unique meaning-making processes and abilities that they use in constructing their knowledge. When they come together as a group to share their independent learning, they expand the pool of knowledge, adding new insights and perceptions for everyone. As they listen to and interact with one another, participants learn about ideas other than their own and begin to assimilate them. At the same time, through the give-and-take of discussion, they come to comprehend and respect how differences of background lead to differences of viewpoint. This process, while ensuring each participant's individuality, connects group members to one another and provides a foundation for building a community of learners.

Several other principles identified in Chapter 1 also contribute to community building: respecting diversity, collaborating, and negotiating. When all of these processes interact, a genuine and productive learning community forms. The teacher memoirs that we recommend later on document how creating a classroom community significantly impacts on the kind and the quality of learning. To better understand this kind of learning we need to delve more deeply.

How Learning Happens—or Doesn't

Theories abound to explain learning from many different perspectives. If you were to search the Web you would find online sources listing numerous learning theories organized in a variety ways. At one site, we found the theories organized under three broad headings: behaviorist, humanistic, and cognitive (www.learningandteaching.info/learning/theories.htm). It is probably fair to say that the behaviorist theories of Ivan Pavlov, B. F. Skinner, Edward L. Thorndike, and John Watson, included on all the lists, were the earliest theories promulgated and are the ones that have been most commonly applied in educational practice. They are the ones advocated by educators who claim that learning must proceed in small steps, that repetition is essential, and that acquiring atomistic skills must precede the study of concepts.

With the contributions of John Dewey, Jean Piaget, Lev Vygotsky, Jerome Bruner, and others, advances in cognitive psychology have broadened our understandings of how people learn. Eleanor Duckworth, in her book *The Having of Wonderful Ideas and Other Essays on Teaching and Learning* (1991), raises readers' consciousness about how they learn and about what it means to know something. With examples drawn from the teaching of science, mathematics, and language, she writes persuasively of her conviction that "the having of wonderful ideas is the essence of intellectual development"(p. 1). She maintains that students should be encouraged toward independent thinking because it will open up numerous possibilities for their inquiry and discovery.

Ellen J. Langer, also a professor of psychology, challenges many of the most popular behaviorist theories and instructional approaches about basic skills, memorization, and delayed gratification. In her book, *The Power of Mindful Learning* (1997), she claims that these strategies produce people who do not learn to think for themselves. Langer's assertions are unsettling because they contradict the ways in which many of us were taught. Because we succeeded in school and earned high grades, we might find it hard to accept the judgment that the quality of our education was not as stellar as we were led to believe.

Among Langer's many foci and experiments concerning how individuals learn, she explores the processes of remembering and forgetting. She claims that forgetting is not necessarily a bad thing:

> We can remember information in two ways: Mindfully or mindlessly. . . . Mindful learning enables us to be sensitive to context and to notice the present. When we have learned information mindfully, we remain open to ways in which information may differ in various situations. This sort of memory may guide our current behavior, as we are primed to notice the subtle changes. When we have learned something mindlessly, however, either by accepting information unconditionally or by overlearning or memorizing it, we may be better off forgetting such context-free facts so that we are not bound to them. (pp. 87–88)

Langer's goal is to cultivate individuals who learn to question what they hear, not only in school but in everyday settings and situations. Through her experiments, Langer illustrates how easily manipulated and conditioned we all are. She demonstrates repeatedly, through stories, fables, and research, that students who are given less direction learn to question and become more flexible learners and problem-solvers. She warns that mindless memorizing often freezes one's ability to grow and change.

> *How do you interpret Langer's theory of mindful learning? In what ways do you agree or disagree with Langer? How does your education hold up in the light of Langer's theories?*

We hope you will see that as your studies and professional experiences progress, the concept of mindful learning will grow from a recurring metaphor to a frequently used lens for analyzing teaching and learning. In this way, you will revisit Langer throughout your reading of this text, using her ideas as a foundation upon which to construct other layers of meaning. As you move on, you should find that Langer's ideas can serve you both as a frame of reference and as an analytical tool.

Another major contribution to understanding the intricacies of learning emerges from Howard Gardner's research on multiple intelligences (MI). Gardner (1985) maintains that individuals differ in the nature of their intelligence and possess specific skills and talents indicative of each type of intelligence. "The mind has the potential to deal with several different kinds of content, but an individual's facility with one content has little predictive power about his or her facility with other kinds of content" (p. xi). Initially, Gardner identified seven intelligences: linguistic, logical-mathematical, spatial, bodily-kinesthetic, musical, interpersonal, and intrapersonal. Recently he added the naturalist intelligence, and he continues to look for others.

Gardner's work has stimulated many educators to pursue the application of MI theory and numerous texts have been published that interpret it. Start by reading online about Gardner and his research on multiple intelligences. We also encourage you to become familiar with his other numerous texts that explore the mind and schooling. Ponder the ramifications of his research and try to reconcile the work of Langer and Gardner.

During the past 20 years studies in brain research and development have provided significant and dramatic contributions to the study of how one learns. Modern technologies such as Magnetic Resonance Imaging (MRI), Positron Emission Tomography (PET), and Electroencephalography (EEG) have enabled scientists to view the brain as it functions, showing detailed areas of activity. For example, studies have shown that during reading, the physical activity of the brain differs for dyslexics and nondyslexics (Bransford et al., 2005). In studying the brain imaging of poor readers, Yale researchers have seen that reading instruction can rewire the brain to enhance learning (Kotulak, 2004). PET scans have discovered that silent reading shows activity in the frontal lobe—an indication of higher-level thinking. Reading aloud activates the motor area of the brain that governs speech. Might this information imply that silent reading is preferable to oral reading (Wolfe, 2001)? Such findings and information hold promise for helping answer many questions and helping to solve numerous teaching and learning problems.

In the meantime, researchers in cognitive psychology, developmental psychology, and neuroscience have shared numerous studies that have created new lenses for viewing learning processes and intellectual development (National Research Council, 2000; Sprenger, 1999; Wolfe, 2001). The latest key findings indicate that learning changes the physical structure of the brain. Structural changes alter the functional organization of the brain; in other words, learning organizes and reorganizes the brain. Different parts of the brain may be ready to learn at different times (National Research Council, p. xvi).

There appears to be a definite relationship between brain development, education, and experience. The more one exercises one's brain, the more one will grow. Neuroscience has clearly shown that the first few years of a child's life are critical to learning and development (Kirp, 2005). Researchers have also learned that both biology and ecology determine learning. Therefore, learning environments must be designed to facilitate a variety of learning processes, the transfer of learning, and competent student performance (National Research Council, 2000). Teachers in all domains must learn to identify and implement those strategies that will best meet the needs of their students, and additionally, they will need to design the settings that will best make this happen. As science begins to unravel the learning process, educators must welcome this information and use it to guide theory and practice. As brain research becomes more and more abundant, the data from these studies must be taken into consideration as the nation's educational systems plan for the future.

How can we build on children's dominant intelligences to enhance and expand their learning capacities? What do you believe is your dominant intelligence? Was it ever recognized in school and in what ways did it support your learning? How might the recent studies on brain research influence your planning and teaching styles?

Who Am I? Who Are We? Why Are We Here?

We also noted in Chapter 1 that autobiography is a useful vehicle for discovering how we came to believe and behave as we do. In his essay, "Autobiography and the Architecture of Self" (1995), William Pinar describes autobiography as "A kaleidoscope of impulses, instincts, memories and dreams . . . visualized, theorized, told as story. . . . It is the task of self-formation, deformation, learning, and unlearning" (pp. 216–217). Going beyond definition to elaboration, he writes:

Autobiography can serve as a method for enlarging, occupying and building the space of meditation. It enlarges the space by pulling back the edges of memory, disclosing more of what has been 'forgotten,' suppressed and denied ... autobiography which makes the self's architecture more complex, moves below the surface of memory requiring the dismantling of self-defenses. . . . It undermines the stories we tell for comfort or amusement sake, and allows (to a variable extent) a re-entry into the past, a re-experience of the past moment now somewhat present in its multidimensionality and orderlessness. Now the edges of memory pulled back, the water and air of experience seep in, making the pool of memory larger, deeper, more complete. (pp. 217–218)

Reconstructing your own learning history has several advantages. First of all, it will show that you already know a great deal about teaching and learning. Second, it will reveal what you believe about teaching and learning. Third, once "you move below the surface of memory" and uncover your experiences, they will become data for your examination, and for comparison. Comparing your memories with those of your colleagues will provide you with a rich source of insights into what people remember and value about their learning.

Preparing a Timeline

We propose that you begin your reflections by creating a "learning autobiography" in the form of a timeline, a visualization of key moments in your learning history. These moments may have occurred at any time or in any place with various individuals in "teacher" roles. What experiences stand out in your memory as you look back at yourself growing up? For example, do you remember learning to tie your shoes, ride a bicycle, or make your bed? Do you remember learning the multiplication tables, learning to love a poem, learning the meaning of friendship, or learning to adapt to new surroundings? This activity is intended to help you see how learning enveloped all aspects of your life and that some of these events profoundly influenced you.

There is no required format for this personal reconstruction. In fact, you are invited to use your imagination, your creativity, your inventiveness, and whatever materials and resources you wish to employ in order to depict those events that you consider important in your learning, whenever and wherever they occurred, in school and out of school. We have seen timelines in the form of calendars, sculptures, clocks, maps, and diaries. They were worked in black and white and in color. Their creators used stick figures and three-dimensional forms. They incorporated photos, artifacts, and music. The possibilities are endless. The main point is to capture your key learning moments and see yourself as a learner.

Creating a Vignette

As the second part of this activity, select one specific learning event from your autobiography and write extensively about it. In looking at your timeline, what moment stands out or sings to you? For example, who gave you the confidence to ride the two-wheeler? What was so memorable about learning to love that poem? What were the circumstances that taught you the meaning of friendship? Write a vignette that describes and examines this snapshot in your learning album. Locate the event in time and space; identify the actors; describe what occurred; show what you learned; analyze why the event was significant in your life.

Think about your unique experience and realize that when you are teaching, each student will also bring a story. How will you use their varied experiences to design your plans and help your students learn more about one another?

Talking, Listening, and Learning

Achieving one of the major goals of inquiring in support of learning depends on a group's ability to engage in meaningful conversation. Making classroom talk productive requires good listening skills, thought, and patience. The purpose is not to reach a single or simple conclusion, but to explore tentative and multiple strands of thought. Exploratory talk (Barnes, 1993) serves as a catalyst, helping teachers and students become better individual speakers and listeners and more effective group participants.

The skills of exploratory talk also contribute to successful collaboration building and ultimately lead to greater achievements in learning. These conclusions are supported by the findings of a three-year study of talk in elementary school classrooms by researchers at the Ontario Institute for Studies in Education. Drawing upon the theories of Vygotsky, Duckworth, and Barnes, Wells and Wells (1992) examine how children construct knowledge together. They conclude:

> In sum, the need for mutual understanding in collaborative talk requires each participant to make his or her meaning clear to the other, and hence also to him- or herself, with the result that thinking is made explicit and thus, available for inspection, and if necessary, for extension, modification, or correction. (p. 61)

Collaborative talk can be as beneficial for teachers and prospective teachers as for elementary, high school, and college students. The studies of Douglas Barnes (1975, 1992) demonstrate that "The more a learner controls his own language strategies, and the more he is enabled to think aloud, the more he can take responsibility for formulating explanatory hypotheses and evaluating them" (p. 29). It is important to note that teachers who have little experience participating in small group discussions will be challenged to run such groups successfully. Teachers as well as students must learn how to develop the skills necessary for group discussion.

Although exploratory talk can be an effective teaching and learning strategy, it is important to note that it can be threatening to students who lack confidence when not speaking in their native language. Such students are hesitant and often unable to participate in class. In addition, some students from other cultures have been taught not to speak in school and not to argue or be contradictory in the classroom (Goldstone, 2000). For them, learning to participate in exploratory talk is a gradual process of learning to adapt to new expectations.

Equally important in any discussion group, therefore, is respecting the silent voices. J. S. Townsend's (1998) *Silent Voices* addresses the complicated dynamics of silence. She identifies that students are quiet for many valid reasons and warns teachers not to assume that these nontalkers are unprepared, disinterested, or bored. Listening might be their greatest skill and they might actually be hard at work. She also suggests strategies to help these students learn to speak out.

Consider your own school experiences. What role did talk play in your learning? When were you most active or passive? Whose voices were valued in your classes? How did silent students participate? How might teachers and peers engage silent students in the learning community?

Narratives on Learning: Other Learners' Stories

Exploring your own and your colleagues' learning histories should have focused your attention on the value of autobiography as a means for understanding individual backgrounds and experience, especially when these are recounted in the first-person voice. Just as this applies to you and your colleagues, it will be applicable to your students. As a teacher you will meet students in your classes whose learning histories are so varied that you will not be able to assume that their experiences were the same as yours. As a prospective teacher, you need to consider that the children you will be teaching will come from diverse backgrounds, have a variety of talents and experiences, and learn in many different ways.

In encouraging the reading of multicultural autobiographical literature, we are informed by the work of Louise Rosenblatt, well known for her transactional approach to the teaching of literature (1938/1965). Rosenblatt maintains that a literary text "remains merely inkspots on paper until a reader transforms them into a set of meaningful symbols. The literary work exists in the live circuit set up between reader and text" (p. 25). Rosenblatt's concept of a literary transaction supports the notion that readers make their own meanings, thereby closely paralleling the constructivist view of the learning process.

Furthermore, Rosenblatt distinguishes between two types of reading stances (1978). She describes the "efferent" reader as one who draws information from the text, and the "aesthetic" reader as the one who engages in a lived through experience with a text. By reading autobiographies, memoirs, and personal narratives, we can experience both types of reading. We can enter into the lives of learners and teachers, while at the same time acquiring knowledge about the learning experiences of young people at different times, in different places, and from different cultures.

Book Groups

We have long been advocates of small group study because we believe that in this environment students are most likely to become active learners as they negotiate and collaborate with their peers. It is interesting for us to note, therefore, that one of the major findings of the 10-year study at Harvard University conducted by Professor Richard L. Light was that the effectiveness of college students' experiences was heightened by their study in groups. "Students who studied on their own and then discussed the work in groups of four to six . . . understood material better and felt more engaged with their classes" (Zernike, 2001).

In the spirit of Light's research, you might wish to form a small study group around a chosen autobiography. Your group should analyze the selection, extracting key themes, exploring the writer's learning experiences, and contemplating the implications of those experiences for teaching and learning.

Book group study and sharing is an approach used in elementary, secondary, and college classrooms, as well as among book-reading adults throughout the country. A critical aspect of group study involves learning to critique how well the group processes are working. To be able to assess the success of group work in your teaching and learning settings, you should regularly explore the following questions:

> *What were the strengths and weaknesses of the way your group functioned? What factors contributed to the group's success? What factors diminished or interfered with the group's success? Did a leader emerge? If so, how and why? Critique your own role as a group member. What did you learn about yourself? What might you and the group do differently next time?*

In Appendix A we have compiled and annotated autobiographies, memoirs, and personal narratives of students and teachers that we have found most valuable over the years. They supplement those we identify here and in Chapter 5. Our search for additions to this list is ongoing, and we welcome suggestions.

Below are the six selections we currently recommend for the small group study of learners. Following each annotation, we pose questions related to the text. Our questions are intended as prompts to expand your purview; they should not limit exploration. For each text, the ultimate question is:

How did the narrator's experiences contribute to his or her development as a learner?

Beals, Melba P. (1994). Warriors Don't Cry. NY: Washington Square Press.

The landmark 1954 Supreme Court ruling in *Brown v. Board of Education* brought the promise of integration to Little Rock, Arkansas, but it was hard-won for the nine black teenagers chosen to integrate Central High School in 1957. Drawn from Melba Beals's personal diaries, this memoir is an account of the experiences she and eight friends had during a year that held no sweet 16 parties or school plays, but that helped shape the civil rights movement.

> *How would you have survived as a member of this group of nine? How do newspapers, history books, and films recount the events in Little Rock then and now? What comparable situations do teenagers face today?*

Chamoiseau, Patrick. (1997). School Days. Lincoln: University of Nebraska Press.

Martinique's Chamoiseau recounts his struggle to keep his identity in a school committed to crushing it. As a little boy, he badgers his mother to let him go to school; later he comes to regret his wish. In the school he attends, the children face a systematic effort to root out the Creole—"po'nigger talk" associated with poverty and subjection—and substitute pure French, the language of Martinique's imperial masters. Sometimes reading like an archetypal narrative of cultural domination, sometimes like an intimate memory from one's childhood, this memoir rewards the effort to learn its language.

> *What was the impact of learning French on Patrick and his friends? What motivated Teacher to act as he did? How might you have reacted and responded as a student in his class? How might these early school experiences have affected Patrick and his classmates' development in school?*

Hickman, Homer H., Jr. (1998). October Sky. NY: Island Books.

It was 1957, the year *Sputnik* raced across the Appalachian sky, and the small town of Coalwood, West Virginia, was slowly dying. Faced with an uncertain future, Homer Hickman nurtured a dream to send rockets into outer space. The introspective son of the mine's superintendent and of a mother determined to get him out of Coalwood forever, Homer fell in with a group of alienated youth who, with support from their teacher, learned not only how to turn scraps of metal into sophisticated rockets, but how to sustain hope in a town that swallowed its men alive.

> *In what ways do the socioeconomic characteristics of the community undermine the boys' goals? How did collaboration among Homer and his peers contribute to their success? How can we help parents understand their role as advocates for their children?*

Kuusisto, Stephen. (1998). Planet of the Blind: A Memoir. NY: Delta.

As a boy he careened down the street on the bicycle his mother bought him. As a teenager he traveled to Europe and played basketball. As a young man he won scholarships, taught classes, and went bird watching. And all the while, Stephen Kuusisto would not utter, even to himself, the one central truth of his life: he could not see. With 20/200 vision in his better eye, he was legally blind. Writes Kuusisto: "I see like a person who looks through a kaleidoscope; my impressions of the world at once beautiful and largely useless." A work of exquisite intelligence and passionate heart, *Planet of the Blind* is for anyone who has viewed the world through a unique lens—and has ultimately seen the truth.

> *How does the word "blind" function as a metaphor in this text? What does Stephen help his readers see? What is the responsibility of a teacher and a class in enabling students with disabilities to become part of the community?*

Lorde, Audre. (1962). Zami; A New Spelling of My Name. Freedom, CA: The Crossing Press.

Zami is a powerful chronicle about a young woman's struggle with her racial and sexual identity and her linkage with the women who shaped her. From her childhood in Harlem to her coming of age in the late 1950s, Lorde shares her journey from a lonely little girl to a troubled adolescent to an independent young woman working to overthrow patriarchal and sexual oppression.

> *How do Audre Lorde's multiple identities interact and impact on her development? How does she deal with issues of social justice? As a teacher, how would you help your students reconcile their personal identities?*

Santiago, Esmeralda. (1993). When I was Puerto Rican. NY: Vintage.

The author's memoir begins in rural Puerto Rico, where she lived with her parents and siblings in a warring, but loving and tender, environment. Santiago describes her past and her transition from her island culture to her bewildering years in New York City. A reviewer for the *Boston Globe* wrote that it "is the bittersweet story of a young girl trapped between two cultures . . . filled with coming-of-age anecdotes and sweet memories of family." How Esmeralda overcame adversity, won acceptance to New York City's High School of Performing Arts, and then went on to Harvard is a record of a tremendous journey by a remarkable woman. This text is also available in Spanish.

> *How does the book's title raise the question of one's identity? How does Esmeralda negotiate life in a new culture? What should teachers learn from Esmeralda's story?*

We hope you will see that autobiographies provide prospective teachers with opportunities to share in the lives of others, similar or dissimilar, to themselves. Although these six selections in no way represent the full diversity of students that teachers will encounter in their classrooms, they powerfully illustrate a range of factors that influence living and learning.

Extending the Conversations: Communicating Online

In education, as in almost every other field, technology is expanding the landscape of how we communicate and how we learn. The use of technology allows classes to communicate as a group beyond their classroom doors. As individuals, students and teachers can widen their circles by entering into chat rooms and discussion boards. The chance to extend conversations provides a continuing opportunity to learn independently and to develop new relationships. For those who are not comfortable speaking aloud, for those who need extra time to organize their thoughts, and for second language learners who are gradually developing their abilities to enter conversations, communicating online is an excellent venue.

Computer technology now offers teachers of children of all ages new opportunities for strengthening their literacy by creating new audiences for them. Chris Davis and Jennifer Davis (2005) describe how their students create their own Web pages, publish oral histories on the Internet, and engage in classroom dialogue online. Liz Kelso (2005) forms student book groups across several classes whose members respond to each other's questions and interpretations. Scott Christian (1997) reports on an online literary exchange on *Anne Frank: Diary of a Young Girl* among middle school students in Alaska, Mississippi, New Mexico, and Vermont.

Reporting on her observations as a college instructor, Erica-lee Lewis writes:

Taking advantage of this different mode of communication has made meeting course goals easier for teachers and students. The use of e mail and Web boards . . . enabled teachers and students to communicate outside the classroom; this provided an additional outlet to discuss problems and pose questions in an expeditious and inclusive way, as an online conversation can involve a throng of students simultaneously. Used as a medium through which unanswered questions and perplexing issues could be posed and addressed by students directly met Inquiries' student-centered, problem-posing mode . . . [and] every aspect of the collaborative model. (in Sobelman, 1999, p. 55)

As a student or as the member of a group of colleagues who are using the computer to communicate, we urge you to adhere to the following guidelines and etiquette:

- Make a habit of checking your email and keeping up with the transactions on a daily basis.
- Be an active participant by contributing your ideas, your questions, and your concerns. Welcome reactions to your views and continue the conversation.
- Respond constructively to the contributions of others. Indicate why you support or disagree with their statements.
- Use clear, concise, and appropriate language.
- Share relevant discoveries from your observations.

- Raise issues from newspaper or television reports. Alert your peers to special events.
- When writing online, remember that a Web board is a public arena.

Our experience in using technology in our courses has had a variety of expected as well as unexpected outcomes. Aside from the sharing of required and daily assignments online, we found that each individual class discovers ways to communicate information that interests and concerns them. They exchange additional citations and knowledge gleaned from other courses, refer to newspaper and magazine articles, and alert each other to forthcoming television documentaries and issue-related programs. Through these various types of communications they expand their learning beyond what occurs in the classroom.

As you become more comfortable with the various ways of communicating via the computer, we encourage you to think about how using a Web board, sharing timelines, and working in study groups could empower your students to take ownership of their learning. As they do so, they will become active members of an expanded learning community.

CHAPTER 3

Knowledge and Knowing

Chapters 2, 3, and 4 are intricately and importantly interlaced. We separate them to tease out the most influential concepts and problematic aspects within each, to highlight how different perspectives lead to different conclusions, and to show how theoretical choices intrude upon the work of teachers and their students.

As we have shown in Chapter 2, numerous theories have been promulgated to explain the learning process and the varied circumstances that define individual learners. But this is not the whole picture. In this chapter, we take into account the differing views of knowledge, what knowledge the schools should be responsible for, and the different ways of knowing that influence how individuals come to uncover and reconstruct knowledge. However, at the same time that we are deciding about knowledge and its representation, we must also attend to the great diversity among those who comprise our school population for whom knowledge grows out of many different experiences and becomes manageable and useful in many different contexts. Therefore, in Chapter 4 we probe those differences that distinguish learners from one another and we raise issues concerning the role of teachers and schools in attending to those differences.

Defining Knowledge

What is knowledge? In its most simplistic and broadest form, knowledge is the information, understandings, skills, and abilities needed to function successfully in the world. Yet, conceptualizing knowledge is far more complex with varied and often contradictory stances on its meaning, acquisition, and application. As we identify some of the different perspectives, we are then obliged to reconcile the relationship between the varying views of knowledge and how they shape ways of knowing.

Philosophers, scholars, and educators have long debated the notion of knowledge, and the positions of some of the current spokespersons are rooted in writings that go back many centuries. While we resist the temptation to review the legacy that shapes the positions held in the 21st century, we will try to shed light on the most influential thinkers operating in and on the educational world of which we are a part.

Perhaps nowhere is the concern about knowledge more convincingly evident than at the college or university level where dedication to the study of the liberal arts, encompassing the natural sciences, the social sciences, and the humanities, is the primary focus. Here, novices are expected to absorb existing knowledge while scholars and researchers strive to create new knowledge. Even at the level of higher education, however, we see great disparities of viewpoint and commitment about what constitutes knowledge and how it should be presented. More relevant to our concerns is that these same practices are now extending downward from the pre-K through high school curricula. For example, standardized testing now begins at age four!

Among the most outspoken advocates at the right end of the knowledge debate continuum are E. D. Hirsch, Jr. (1988, 1996) and Diane Ravitch and Chester Finn (1988). In their indictments of public education, they argue against the premise that knowledge is changing and that progressive school reform is necessary. They maintain that schools should offer a solid core of knowledge that is unchanging, including the basic principles of science and government, the essential elements of mathematics, and the fundaments of oral and written language.

In addition, they are strong supporters of state and national standards accompanied by rigorous testing. Whether they invoke the term "back to basics," "core knowledge," "cultural literacy," the "canon," or "moral values and virtues," they all claim democratic intent. They believe that all students are entitled to a common curriculum, that the schools should represent the values of the founding fathers, and that all learners should be held accountable to the same high expectations.

While there is a great temptation to reject outright the position of these conservers of knowledge, labeling as inert the knowledge they defend, the real challenge is to interrogate the ideas and content they espouse and, where appropriate, reframe that knowledge so that it is relevant for our present society. An early example of this approach is found in the work of the philosopher Alfred North Whitehead (1949):

> In particular, so long as we conceive intellectual education as merely consisting in the acquisition of mechanical mental aptitudes, and of formulated statements of useful truths, there can be no progress; though there will be much activity, amid aimless re-arrangement of syllabuses, in the fruitless endeavor to dodge the inevitable lack of time. We must take it as an unavoidable fact . . . that there are more topics desirable for knowledge than any one person can possibly acquire. . . . What I am anxious to impress is that though knowledge is one chief aim of intellectual education, there is another ingredient, vaguer but greater, and more dominating in its importance. The

ancients called it "wisdom." You cannot be wise without some basis of knowledge, but you may easily acquire knowledge and remain bare of wisdom. (pp. 40–41)

Whitehead also clarifies the relationship between knowledge and wisdom: "It concerns the handling of knowledge, its selection for the determination of relevant issues, its employment to add value to our immediate experience" (p. 41). It appears to us that educators must continue to keep Whitehead's vision alive and not limit the ways in which students perceive and interpret knowledge. It is important that we maintain the spirit that led our pioneers to cross the country, cure diseases, expand technology, and land on the moon.

Forty years later, a compelling case for "transforming knowledge" from a feminist perspective is articulated by Elizabeth Minnich (1990). She maintains that the knowledge tradition has been limited to the ideas and dispositions of White Euro-American males. Minnich examines four kinds of conceptual errors that she believes have reinforced the dominant tradition: faulty generalizations, circular reasoning, mystified concepts, and partial knowledge. Although all four of her concepts are worthy of discussion, for our purposes we focus on the partial knowledge category, where she explains: "Beyond any particular body of accepted knowledge are the definitions, the boundaries established by those in power" (p. 151). There is a void of those not in power because the voices and the works of women and of racially, socially, and economically marginalized groups have been notably omitted from the discourse. "The construction of knowledge has thereby lost not only whole realms of subject matter but modes of thought and populations of people whose knowledge was not 'the same' as the defining, ordering kind" (p. 152). Educators must help students see and hear the voices of all those who live in places unfamiliar to them. Minnich concludes her lengthy analysis with a simple reminder:

We cannot now . . . either ignore exclusivity or transmute it into inclusiveness. The "simple" matter of pronouns contains the whole of our problem, and there is no shortcut to fixing it. Every time we stumble over a pronoun, we stumble over the root problem that entangles the dominant tradition in its own old errors. (p. 175)

Another group of educators continues to challenge the "dominant tradition" theory. They are the proponents of a critical pedagogy "designed to serve the purpose of both empowering teachers and teaching empowerment (where pedagogy and culture are seen as intersecting fields of struggle" (McLaren, 1989, p. x). Deeply relevant to this perspective is Paulo Freire's (1970) condemnation of the banking approach to teaching and learning that views students as being oppressed and prevented from acting on their world. The views of Henry Giroux (1988) add further dimension to critical pedagogy theory. Like Freire, Giroux sees knowledge as a powerful tool to be used to induce change and improve the human condition. In contrasting productive and directive knowledge he contends:

Productive knowledge is primarily concerned with means . . . productive knowledge is instrumental. . . . Directive knowledge is a mode of inquiry designed to answer questions that productive inquiry cannot answer; it is concerned with speculative questions centering around the relationship between means and ends . . . in which students question the purpose of what they are learning. It is knowledge that questions how productive knowledge is to be used. Directive knowledge formulates the most important questions in improving the quality of life because it asks "For what end?" (p. 49)

Undoubtedly the knowledge debate will continue, but caught in the middle are hundreds of thousands of teachers and school administrators who struggle to strike a balance. They must find the means to accommodate to arbitrary standards and enable all students to satisfy an array of assessments and evaluations. They must strive to respect the varying needs and differences among children, adolescents, families, and communities. Most important, they must honor their students as learners and devise all possible opportunities to promote and engage their students in using knowledge for critical and creative thinking.

Arno Bellack (1965), echoing the question of the philosopher and early sociologist Herbert Spencer (1911), also asked "What Knowledge Is of Most Worth?" At the time Bellack was writing, he was particularly concerned about an overemphasis on the structure of individual disciplines. He worried that there was a neglect of efforts to draw together the common characteristics within and among groups of disciplines so they might serve human affairs. Answering Bellack's question today is far more challenging. The overwhelming accumulation of information, compounded by the integration of 21st-century technology, adds even greater complexity to how we think about, organize, study, and interpret knowledge.

In his work, Barnes (1992) presents a framework for educational practitioners that divides knowledge into two categories, *school knowledge* and *action knowledge*. Barnes is concerned that knowledge not lay dormant, but that students be able to transform knowledge for useful purposes:

School knowledge is the knowledge which someone else presents to us. We partly grasp it, enough to answer the teacher's questions, to do exercises, or to answer examination questions, but it remains someone else's knowledge. If we never use this knowledge we probably forget it. In so far as we use knowledge for our own purposes however we begin to incorporate it into our view of the world, and to use parts of it to cope with the exigencies of living. Once the knowledge becomes incorporated into that view of the world on which our actions are based, I would say that it becomes "action knowledge." (p. 81)

Among a teacher's many challenges is striving to balance "school knowledge" with what matters most to students. Although students must be prepared for the mandated assessments, this does not mean that teaching and learning should be passive or devoid of personal meaning. Despite the pressures for accountability, teachers can ignite their students' passion to want to know. When students raise questions and seek answers to what they care about, the combination of their curiosity, critical thinking skills, and intrinsic desire to learn and understand creates its own energy. To harness that energy we must tap into yet another set of skills, the personal and interpersonal skills that are the foundation for self-knowledge and the building of relationships. This knowledge, the ability to work and play well with others, should be recognized as a standard to be reached.

So, we ask again: "What is knowledge?" We have tried to show that the conventional definitions stress the content of the disciplines and that even the less traditional ones only obliquely suggest that there are additional kinds of knowledge for which schools are held responsible. Yet, as the major socializing agency, schools are expected to ensure that students know how to interact effectively with peers and adults, engage in both independent and collaborative activities, be motivated and self-directed, participate appropriately in diverse learning settings and communities, respect and enhance the environment, and maintain healthful habits of mind and body. While these skills and attitudes may not be measurable on a scantron, they are measurable in the moment-to-moment interactions that take place each day. They represent the necessary "basics" for acquiring and using the accumulated knowledge of the ages and for daily living in the real world.

Where do you see yourself on the knowledge continuum? What kinds of knowledge do you most value? How do you see your beliefs about knowledge influencing your role as a teacher?

How Do We Know What We Know?

Perhaps even more difficult than deciding how to define knowledge is reconciling the many explanations for the process of knowing. A good transition in this regard is the connection Dewey makes between knowledge and thinking (1910/1997). For Dewey:

... genuine knowledge always consists in part in the discovery of something not understood in what had previously been taken for granted as plain, obvious, matter-of course, and in part in the use of meanings that are directly grasped without question, as instruments for getting hold of obscure, doubtful, and perplexing meanings. (p. 120)

What we call "knowing" for Dewey is "thinking," a process of reflection entailing active, persistent, and careful consideration of any belief or supposed form of knowledge in the light of the grounds that support it, and the further conclusions to which it tends (p. 6). Dewey argues that thinking requires the application of the scientific method and is dependent on human interaction. He emphasizes that it is "futile to expect a child to evolve a universe out of his own mere mind. . . . It is the development of experience and into experience that is really wanted" (Dewey, 1990/1900/1902, p. 18). Students must construct and reconstruct concepts and ideas. Dewey explains through the metaphor of an explorer who blazes a trail and creates a map of unchartered territory. Others are then able to use this map and compare their own wanderings:

But the map, a summary, an arranged and orderly view of previous experiences, serves as a guide to future experience; it gives direction; it facilitates control; it economizes effort, preventing useless wandering, and pointing out the paths which lead most quickly and most certainly to a desired result. Through the map every new traveler may get for his own journey the benefits and results of others' explorations. . . (p. 20)

The teacher's role is to tap into the child's own references and "determine the medium in which the child should be placed in order that his growth may be properly directed. He is concerned, not with the subject matter as such, but with the subject matter as a related factor in a total and growing experience" (p. 201). Dewey constantly reminds us that the child is a "scientist" and that knowledge is built, explored, and deeply internalized—not memorized.

In a similar vein, Jerome Bruner, one of today's foremost cognitive and developmental psychologists, has written extensively about the process of knowing. Bruner strongly believes that skills and ideas must be taught in a broad, organized context to help students connect and transfer knowledge they already have in related areas. Teaching skills and ideas in isolation deprives students of the organization they need to retrieve and process information meaningfully. Bruner (1960) contends that knowledge is created through the act of discovery. He believes that students should be active learners and that teachers should function in a hypothetical mode, helping students navigate ways to problem solve. Engaging students in the inquiry process creates discovery that "is in its essence a matter of rearranging or transforming evidence in such a way that one is enabled to go beyond the evidence so reassembled to additional new insights" (p. 402). He continues, "Our aim as teachers is to give our students as firm a grasp of a subject we can, and to make him as autonomous and self-propelled a thinker as we can—one who will go along on his own after formal schooling has ended" (p. 403).

Bruner is also noted for creating the idea of a spiral curriculum, in which a theme is introduced and revisited regularly throughout students' educational careers. As students grow and gain experience in the world, they build new ideas that help expand and transform their old ones. As students revisit these themes with new perspectives, this "spiraling" creates a deeper and more meaningful understanding of the topic at hand. The constructivist perspectives of psychologists Jean Piaget and Lev Vygotsky are indebted to Dewey's seminal work and to Bruner's wide-ranging analyses.

Jean Piaget (1896–1960), a Swiss-born psychologist, is renowned for developing the theory of cognitive development. His research focused on how children construct knowledge, solve problems, and make sense of the world. Piaget was also one of the first to understand that children and adults view the world very differently. Piaget's studies led to the development of stage theory, which describes all children as progressing through four sequential stages of development: sensorimotor period, ages 0–two; preoperational period, ages two–seven; concrete operations, ages seven–eleven; and formal operations, ages eleven–fifteen. Piaget determined that as children interacted with their environment, learning and development occurred. He also identified benchmark behaviors that moved children from one stage to the next.

Because Piaget saw children as active learners who through their interactions were always constructing and reconstructing their view of the world, his theory is known as constructivist theory. He observed that children learned from one another, especially in multiage groups, and therefore determined that learning should be child-centered and activity-based. Teachers who work with young children should be aware of cognitive development, should know their students well, and should provide them with activities and experiences that are developmentally appropriate.

Lev Vygotsky (1896–1934), a Russian psychologist, introduced the sociocultural theory of child development. In his book, *Mind in Society* (1978), he writes, "From the very first days of the child's development, his activities acquire a meaning of their own in a system of social behavior and, being directed towards a definite purpose, are refracted through the prism of the child's environment" (p. 30). According to Vygotsky, children grow and develop by interacting with those in their world. He also discovered that children use language internally and externally to explain the world around them, thereby developing higher order thinking processes. In essence, when children seem to be talking to themselves, they are often explaining and making sense of what they are doing. Vygotsky's biggest contribution to the field of developmental psychology was his concept of the zone of proximal development. This is described as the distance between actual and potential development—what a child can do independently and what a child can do with support and expert guidance (p. 86). A teacher who works closely with children should know when a child is ready to move on. He or she can take advantage of a child's readiness or create an environment with other capable children to enable the child to take the next step.

The theories of both Piaget and Vygotsky concern cognitive development and learning. The essential difference is that Piaget's theory, called cognitive constructivism, focuses on the individual's construction in the learning process whereas Vygotsky's theory, referred to as social constructivism, emphasizes the social and cultural contexts in which learning occurs.

Preparing to teach requires serious study of human development and the theories that influence learning. Science has already shown us that subject matter cannot become internalized by straight lecture or rote memorization. How you as a professional approach teaching is far more important than what you are teaching.

How does constructivism, both as an individual cognitive approach and as a social, interactive approach, inform your thinking about the teaching-learning process? How do you see implementing these approaches in your classroom?

Naming and Labeling

For the most part, teachers' knowledge falls into four categories: the things they know, the things they don't know, the things they don't know that they know, and the things they don't know they don't know. For example, most teachers are knowledgeable about the content they are expected to teach but may not know appropriate strategies to help their students learn that content. Many teachers are unaware of the heroic lengths they would go to protect their students in an emergency and often do not know the degree to which their reactions to their students may be hurtful and demeaning.

Of all the issues teachers and prospective teachers face, the one they find most conflicting is coming to terms with their own knowledge, feelings, and attitudes toward people different from themselves. Lisa Delpit refers to this as learning to teach "other people's children" (Delpit, 1995). Teachers often don't know how their upbringing and personal beliefs directly affect their actions in the classroom. Typically, most of their previous classroom experiences took place in the homogeneous schools they attended while they were growing up. Until faced with a sea of unfamiliar faces representing a variety of cultures, many teachers do not realize that they harbor biases, fears, stereotypical beliefs, and misunderstandings about others. They are often unprepared to address the challenges that diversity poses. Admittedly, the range of differences among their students can be overwhelming, including as it does race, class, gender, culture, language, religion, sexual orientation, age, ability, and disability. Yet, until teachers take responsibility for facing themselves, confronting their feelings, and examining their beliefs honestly, they are likely to flounder in building the necessary constructive relationships with their peers, their students, and their students' families. These unidentified and often unrecognizable personal traits deeply embedded within one's knowing are the foci of this chapter.

Despite the overwhelming challenge that issues of diversity raise, there seem to be few occasions in most of our early schooling for uncovering assumptions and studying about individual differences. Over the years, our former students have told us that although they found studying the topic of diversity discomfiting, even emotionally draining, they welcomed being able to explore and discuss this complicated and provocative subject in the safety of the Inquiries community. Many students acknowledged that the readings and classroom exchanges helped them acquire new perspectives and sharpened their awareness of their beliefs and their behaviors as they relate to classroom dynamics and to identity politics. In raising this often "hidden and forbidden" topic, we are challenging you to search for a deeper understanding of who you are and begin learning more about your peers, the students you are meeting in your field placements, and in time, your future students. Although no single book, article, or course can fully explore all of the issues and problems that prospective teachers are likely to face, we see this chapter as providing a key to opening a door that is often marked "off limits."

Identity and Identity Politics: Labels Are Us

In 1988, Peggy McIntosh, at the Wellesley College Center for Research on Women, published a groundbreaking paper, "White Privilege and Male Privilege: A Personal Account of Coming to See Correspondences Through Work in Women's Studies." This analysis and its shorter form "White Privilege and Male Privilege: Unpacking the Invisible Knapsack" (1989), now available online at the Peggy McIntosh Web site, has been instrumental in putting the dimension of privilege into discussions of gender, race, class, and sexuality in the United States and around the world.

In a press release from Oberlin College in March 2001, (http//:www.Oberlin.edu/ newserv O1 mar/peggy_mcintosh_release html), McIntosh is quoted as saying:

> Oppression can take active forms, which we see, and embedded forms, which as members of the dominant group in society one is taught not to see. I was taught to see racism only in individual acts of meanness, not an invisible system conferring dominance on my group from birth.

Just as McIntosh was astounded by the discovery of her own invisible racism, her work awakens others of dominant cultures to reflect on their identity and how their privileged position has influenced the direction of their lives. Acknowledging the invisibility factor often reveals how naive we are in understanding the connection between identity and identity politics. While many of us do not perceive ourselves as elevated in status, McIntosh reminds us that our various identities automatically place us, or do not place us, in positions of power and authority. Furthermore, for those who are part of the dominant culture, confronting their identity means accepting the fact that the privileges enjoyed are theirs by virtue of belonging to the group in power. Many people are either unaware of their privileges or simply take them for granted, until they encounter McIntosh's list of 26 identifiers of White privilege, which shockingly brings this to their attention. You might wish to begin your study of identity and identity politics by looking at McIntosh's list to see where you stand relative to her list of identifiers.

The issue of privilege, however, is but a single dimension of the broader configuration of racism haunting our society and, therefore, our schools. Learning and talking about racism and developing strategies to overcome the barriers of resistance to studying about racism have become focal points in the work of Beverly Daniel Tatum. In her article "Talking About Race, Learning About Racism: The Application of Racial Identity Development Theory in the Classroom" (1992), Tatum introduces a series of working assumptions about racism and describes the stages of racial development as they relate separately to Black and White populations. Drawing on Cross's model of Black racial identity development (1971, 1978, 1991), Tatum presents her five stages of the development process: preencounter, encounter, immersion/emersion, internalization and internalization-commitment. She also presents her students with Helms's model of White racial identity development (1990): contact, disintegration, reintegration, pseudo-independence, immersion/emersion, and autonomy. Her article is important because it presents both perspectives for exploration and puts in place a process for personal and group study.

Tatum uses her own college classroom and her students' responses to further study the issues. She devises a set of rules to guide the discussion. Because the issues generated are emotionally charged, often rendering feelings of anger, confusion, and resistance, Tatum maintains it is critical to facilitate an open yet supportive environment to help guide attitude changes among students. It isn't until students make this discovery that they can act on it and begin to take responsibility. Tatum stresses that "Heightening students' awareness of racism without an understanding of the possibilities of change is a prescription for despair." Moreover, she says, "it is unethical to do one without the other" (p. 20). The ultimate goal of her work is to empower her students to become agents of change who will work productively to address issues of racism in positive ways. Although Tatum focuses specifically on race, she notes that other issues of oppression, such as anti-Semitism, homophobia, and ageism, fall into the domain for exploring differences. The work of McIntosh and Tatum raise questions that every teacher and prospective teacher should try to answer.

> *In what ways do you see yourself as privileged or not privileged? Can members of nondominant groups be privileged and racist? If you were a student in Tatum's classroom, how would you feel about exploring these issues with your peers? How does the work of Tatum and McIntosh help you define yourself and your responsibility as an agent of change in the social, economic, and political arenas? What are the implications of their messages for you as a prospective teacher and as an ongoing learner?*

Keith Gilyard's Story

In *Voices of the Self* (1991), for which he received an American Book Award, Keith Gilyard gives us two books within the covers of one. In alternating chapters you can read his autobiographical account of his growing up in New York as an African-American male and his description and analysis of the ways in which language variation, culture, and school success intersect.

The stories Gilyard recounts of his experiences in school and community forcefully depict the prejudice and ignorance he faced as a Black child and youth. In his bold, honest, and personal chronicle, he recounts his developing two personas in order to navigate the cultural divide in which he existed. He learned at an early age that his intelligence and abilities benefited him in school and in settings of the dominant culture. Yet, these strengths were not always valued on his home turf. One of the strategies Gilyard used to preserve his identity was *code switching,* which he had learned from his mother. This is a strategy by which speakers move from their home language to the dominant language of the community. His way of coping was to become Raymond in the classroom and on the playground, and Keith in his home and among others of his race.

It is hard for any reader to escape the truths Gilyard unveils about social structures and identity politics, and about the prevailing attitudes and values permeating schools and classrooms. His narrative alerts us to the deeply complex and entrenched barriers facing African Americans, from their unique history to how their children learn. His stories are representative of the struggles encountered by many students who are not of the dominant culture. As immigrant groups continue to arrive in the United States, Gilyard forces us to ask questions about how the same issues of race, culture, and history impact on learners of other groups. How is it the same or different for Latinos from different countries, for Asians whose identities are connected to places as different as China, Japan, India, or Korea, or for people of the Caribbean whose histories, languages, and religions vary from island to island?

It's Much More Than Ebonics

Researchers have confirmed that Ebonics, considered the informal speech of many African Americans, is indeed a language. According to John R. Rickford (1997), the Linguistic Society of America has described Ebonics as "systematic and rule-governed like all natural speech varieties." In his article, "Suite for Ebony and Phonics," originally published in *Discover* magazine (1997), Rickford provides an historical grounding and clear explanation of the elements that define Ebonics as a language. Ebonics, he says, "includes distinctive patterns of pronunciations and grammar, the elements of language on which linguists tend to concentrate. . . ." And, he continues, "Ebonics is more of a dialect of English than a separate language, insofar as it shares most of its vocabulary and many other features with other informal varieties of American English, and insofar as its speakers can understand and be understood by speakers of most other American English dialects." We encourage you to locate Rickford's paper and read it in its entirety (http://www.stanford.edu/~rickford/papers/SuiteForEbonyAndPhonics.html).

While not negating the political dimensions of the Ebonics controversy, Gilyard moves beyond politics to focus on the linguistic and pedagogical aspects. His gift is thrusting the reader into the continuing debates about language competence as it relates to standard English and to Black English. In an address (1993) to an audience of educators, he spoke on the topic, "Language Learning and Democratic Development." Teaching at Medgar Evers College at that time, he reflected on the effect a deficit model had on his students:

> Deviations from standard or target usage are treated as deficiencies. Black English is "broken English" and has to be repaired. Jamaican Creole is "broken English" and has to be operated upon. There is a line on the back of the City University of New York Writing Assessment Test booklet on which students are to indicate their native language. Many students from the Caribbean indeed write "broken English" on this line. The first few times I saw this I thought the students were being facetious, but I soon changed my mind. The rate at which they were failing the exam was no joke. Students, not dialects, have been broken, and negative responses to language differences have been much of their problem. An equality model of language variation, the only one supported by modern sociolinguistic scholarship, would not support repair models of instruction. (p. 5)

In this statement, Gilyard documents how members of nondominant cultures are led to believe that their speech is substandard, reflecting their ignorance, their lack of education, and their inability to accommodate to the acceptable norms. He goes on to explain:

> Writing instruction in schools has much to do with standards set by powerful groups. Being able to produce texts that meet that standard may be a valuable ability; however, a focus on the standard to be reached, accompanied by disregard for different ways students may try to get there, is authoritarian and disabling. (p. 6)

Gilyard's contributions to our knowledge base are multiple. He shares his childhood perspectives on how he perceived the world and how he thought the world perceived him. He makes it possible for us to see the world through his eyes and to hear his many voices as he struggles to come to terms with his worlds. He shows us the critical role race, language, and culture play in an individual's life.

Although we have focused on Gilyard's text, he is one among many scholars who addresses these critical issues. Henry Louis Gates, Jr. (2004) maintains that the need to be successful does not mean one must abandon one's identity:

> . . . it isn't a derogation of the Black vernacular—a marvelously rich and inventive tongue—to point out that there's a language of the marketplace, too, and learning to speak that language has generally been a precondition for economic success, whoever you are. When we let Black youth become monolingual, we've limited their imaginative and economic possibilities. (p. 11)

It is our responsibility as educators to convey to our students that speaking standard English and succeeding academically should not be viewed as selling out. The hard work it takes to get there must not be minimized. The opportunity to make the choices that can changes one's life oc-cur most often when one has the motivation, tools, and support to succeed (Cochran-Smith, 1995; Delpit, 1995; Ladson-Billings, 1994; Nieto, 1999, 2000; Sleeter & Grant, 1999).

Can you remember incidents where you have witnessed code switching in action? Can you identify code switching in your own life? As a prospective classroom teacher, how might you address the various language patterns of your students? How do you reconcile enabling students to meet educational standards while preserving their language identity?

Diversity in Its Many Manifestations

Although McIntosh, Tatum, and Gilyard do not explicitly relate issues of privilege and identity to all of the different groups within our society, by extension we can recognize the im-plications of their work for many others whose identities are tied to particular characteristics. It is beyond the limits of this text to address in detail the problems and disputes associated with the needs of each group, but it is important to declare that the differences exist, that they should be respected, and that they impact significantly on teaching and learning.

Social Class Differences

Many scholars concerned with socioeconomic differences have noted the intricate interplay of race, class, and gender. When brought down to the realities of a classroom in a particular school and community, this combination of differences can be brutal (Verdi, 2000). Family relationships, parental attitudes, child-rearing patterns, and the value placed on education are influential deter-minants reflecting social class differences. Children and adolescents become the targets of depri-vations, comparisons, and what Jonathan Kozol calls "savage inequalities" (1991). Parents and caregivers can protect their children only so much because when they enter the circles outside the home they are fair game. What a child wears, how a child speaks, what a child brings for lunch, the amount of pocket change a child may have, and where a child lives all impact on how that in-dividual is received by others. Migrant children, immigrant children, and homeless children are examples of students who most obviously fall into this category. "A Plague for the Young Home-less," a short piece on the editorial page of the *New York Times* (March 3, 2004, A18), reports on the high incidence of chronic asthma among New York City's homeless children. "Low income living environments are often the perfect hosts for long-irritating particles, like dust, sooty air, and the waste of household pests. Unhealthy nutrition is a co-conspirator."

While disputes rage about support for welfare, free lunches, medical care, and other so-cial programs, teachers are left without the basic resources to protect their students' physical, emotional, and intellectual growth and development.

Sexual Orientation Differences

With very few exceptions, our schools, mirroring the larger society in which they are situated, have yet to make serious efforts to meet the needs of gay, lesbian, bisexual, and transgender students, parents, and teachers. Although precise statistics are not available, there are too many reported incidents of harassment, rejection, psychological breakdown, and suicide, and too many unsafe schools, for us not to raise questions about the suffering compounded daily. In addition, the continuing concerns about the AIDS epidemic further exacerbate homophobic behavior, creating tensions that may lead to violence.

Family units consisting of two mothers or two fathers suffer as well. Attempts to legalize their status as married have become front-page news as states battle the moral and constitutional issues. In most cases, a general lack of understanding and long-held biases cause these families to be viewed as unacceptable. Although some children in gay or lesbian families adjust well, others struggle to accept their situation. Some children find themselves rejected and others are unable to develop and maintain friendships.

Some cities have created separate schools to protect, respect, and ensure students' rights to a public education, and other schools are developing programs and clubs that acknowledge and include these students. For all students, but especially for gay and lesbian students, schools must be safe and accepting places.

Religious Differences

Largely ignored is public education's increasing dilemma about how to respond to the religious beliefs held by different members of our society. It would appear that this topic is seen as beyond the realm of educational decision makers, yet schools are populated by students who are unable to participate in a variety of events that conflict with their cultural beliefs. Occasionally the issues of the recitation of the Pledge of Allegiance, prayer in the schools, the teaching of evolution, the censorship of selected texts, or the wearing of head coverings and religious symbols reach the national stage; most commonly, they are debated locally, isolated to the particular communities where discord arises. While some of these contests have led to judicial actions and political infighting, clear guidelines concerning these issues have not been articulated. What is even more disheartening is that there exists a lack of baseline cross-cultural knowledge and tolerance of different religious beliefs and practices across our nation and around the world, the outcome of which is evident in international tensions and wars.

Language Differences

The conflicts over bilingualism, registered in voting booths across our country, as well as in our schools, leave most teachers without the guidance they need. They are constantly faced with new students entering their classrooms who have limited or no English proficiency. Many strategies have been adopted to address this issue, but research findings are contradictory and inconclusive. Different states have adopted different mandates, often causing divisiveness within communities. In California, the citizenry voted to cancel bilingual programs and prohibit teachers from communicating in any language other than English. In other states, dual language and immersion programs continue to be implemented, but they are always under the threat of cancellation, and "English Only" proponents are growing in number.

Although our country continues to welcome immigrants, newcomers face painful adjustments as their heritages and customs are often ignored. Children come to school willing and able to learn, but as second language learners their academic potential is not recognized and their progress is impeded through no fault of their own. The assumption that one year of special English classes will suffice is contradicted by the research of scholars in the field of second language acquisition.

As the immigrant populations continue to grow and stabilize, they have begun to raise their voices as to how they want their children to be educated. Whereas states and cities customarily have taken responsibility for the arbitrary placement of immigrant children in bilingual, dual language, or immersion classes, parents are becoming more vocal and want their preferences heard.

Gender Differences

Confusion and arguments over how to respond to gender differences among children and youth in our schools continue unabated and unresolved. Substantial research conducted under the auspices of the American Association of University Women, and compelling classroom studies exemplified by Sadker and Sadker (1994), reveal that schools shortchange girls and that inequalities persist. Boys are called on more often than girls, are allowed to dominate classroom discussions, and are less likely to be reprimanded for calling out. Although the stereotypical image of girls as "Barbie dolls" and models of femininity has somewhat abated, the perception that girls are less able than boys to handle advanced studies in science and mathematics still exists.

The extensive body of research focusing on girls over the past 20 years has led to heightened interest and research on boys. Although adolescent boys seem to test better than girls in math and science, greater numbers of boys are labeled with learning disorders, autism, and attention deficit disorder. There is a growing recognition that boys are deeply affected by society's mixed messages about how they should behave, and many find themselves stuck in a "gender straitjacket." The "macho" expectations to which they are held often result in many young men living behind a mask of masculine bravado and hiding expressions of sensitivity and caring (Pollack, 1998).

The jury may still be out on whether or not there should be separate schools for boys and girls, but there is little doubt that developing the right balance in school curricula and school policies has a long way to go.

Age Differences

Almost totally ignored is any genuine regard for the age differences among students, perhaps most evident at the post secondary level. Although there is a body of research and theory about adulthood and adult learning styles, neither is given much credence in the curriculum and instructional approaches used with nontraditional-aged students. As this population continues to grow, it includes immigrant families seeking the rewards that learning promises. As parents, they want to be able to support and understand their children's educational and developmental needs. Community-based programs and institutions of higher education are obliged to address adults' ways of knowing, and how adults' needs, interests, concerns, aspirations, and diverse cultures influence their learning.

And So Many Other Differences

The categories discussed thus far are not all-inclusive. There are other differences among learners that also require a teacher's awareness and sensitivity: children of divorced parents; children with a single parent; orphaned children; adopted children; children living in shelters; migrant children; refugee children; children with seriously ill or disabled parents. These children, as well as many others, are dealing with new relationships, uncertainty, dislocation, and disruption; their schooling has been affected by circumstances beyond their control and beyond the classroom.

Thus, though we talk about a fair and democratic country, honoring diversity remains a formidable task. Despite the laws safeguarding religious freedom, protecting voting rights, ensuring equality of opportunity, eliminating segregation, and requiring accommodations for the handicapped, many in our society are abused by racism, religious bias, male chauvinism, ridicule, homophobia, and discrimination. Ironically, to a great extent, the responsibility for helping people overcome their ignorance and their prejudice falls to teachers, themselves often neither secure in their beliefs nor fully prepared to deal with these controversies.

Abilities and Disabilities: A Case of Success and Contention

The arena where differences have received the most attention is associated with exceptional children, students with special abilities or disabilities. The complexity and controversy surrounding this subject has resulted in the passage of significant federal, state, and local legislation, the history of which is rooted in the civil rights struggles of the 1950s and 1960s. At the turn of the 20th century, public education still excluded students of color and students with disabilities from attending school. The mandate for compulsory education and the decision of *Brown v. Board of Education* opened the public school doors for these children (Ferguson, 1996) for the first time. However, the opportunity to attend public schools did not mean these students were treated fairly or that they received an education equal to those of their more "normal" peers.

Labeling and Mislabeling

These students were products of "functional exclusion" (Turnbull, 1986), in which those with severe disabilities were most often placed in separate and isolated classrooms or in special schools away from the mainstream. Students with milder disabilities were placed in regular classrooms where they rarely received a differentiated curriculum or the needed instructional attention. Their inability to succeed often caused them to be labeled as "slow learners" or "disciplinary problems." Although a sparse number of special education programs did exist, these children found themselves in segregated classes and classrooms and were labeled as "mentally retarded," "crippled," or "emotionally disturbed" (Heward & Cavanaugh, 1993). On the other end of the spectrum, little information was known about gifted and talented children, and it was simply assumed that students with special talents and abilities would fare well in regular classes and require no additional guidance, instruction, or support.

The past 30 years have brought about numerous changes in the field of special education, which flourished in response to the civil rights movement of the 1950s and 1960s. Parents of exceptional children began to question the concept of isolation in special schools and exclusion from regular education classes. Statistics also began to reveal that large numbers of children, especially boys from non-White and non-English speaking cultures, were being labeled and moved into special education classes. By the 1970s, highly vocal parents, educators, and civil rights activists began to create advocacy groups and file lawsuits to prevent continuing discrimination. They highlighted the issues of excluding exceptional children from regular classes, providing an ineffective and inappropriate education for those enrolled in regular classes, and classifying designated students as having disabilities who essentially had none (Turnbull, Turnbull, Shank, & Leal, 1999). Parents and advocates strongly protested the use of intelligence tests as the determinant for placing children in special classes, the practice of not testing children in their native languages, and arguments provided by public schools that educating exceptional students was too expensive (Heward & Cavanaugh, 1993). The combination of numerous, hard-fought court cases and extremely powerful and influential advocacy finally resulted in the sweeping federal legislation reform of 1975, PL 94–142, the Education for All Handicapped Children Act.

Landmark Legislation

PL 94–142 mandates that all children ages five to 21, regardless of the severity and type of their disabilities, be provided with a "free, appropriate public education," emphasizing special education and related services designed to meet their unique needs. The legislation clearly spells out the roles of parents, teachers, and administrators and designates that students be placed in the "least restrictive environment." Exceptional children no longer could be denied access to educational opportunities. Amendments to the law in 1983 and 1986 expanded research and services, provided increased funding to certain programs, and added special educational services to children three to five years of age. Despite the additions and improvements built into this legislation, the needs of many children were still not being met.

In 1990, the law was expanded and reissued as PL 101–476, the Individuals with Disabilities Education Act, IDEA, which mandated all children and youth a free, appropriate, and public education regardless of the type or severity of their disabilities. Children with multiple and more severe disabilities were being allowed to enter the mainstream. However, further study by congressional committees and research findings made public by the National Council in Disability in 1995 called for still additional improvements to the law. IDEA was strengthened and reissued in 1997 as PL 105–17, a comprehensive law so multifaceted it was divided into several parts. Part A covers the law's purposes and policies to be enacted; Part B, the rights of students between the ages of three to 21; and Part C, the rights of infants and toddlers from birth through age two. The 2004 reauthorization of IDEA, PL 108–446, created a new shift in policy that has created an outcry from within the special education community. The items in question include qualifications of special education teachers, assessment of special education students, and disciplinary procedures regarding special education students. It will be important to see how national, state, and special education agencies clarify and resolve these issues.

Interestingly, PL94–142 did not include provisions for gifted and talented children. Separate legislation was enacted to meet their needs. The Gifted and Talented Children's Act of 1978, PL 95–561, provided financial incentives to those state and local education agencies that wished to develop programs to further support the growth and development of these students. These monies also included funding for teacher inservice development and research. Various changes in federal agencies led to revisions in funding and by 1982 states received block grants to support gifted children. Many states were slow to participate in this process. The most important gains came in 1988 with the passage of the Elementary and Secondary Education Act. This legislation included the Jacob K. Javits Gifted and Talented Student Education Act and provided $8 million to identify gifted and talented children, provide them appropriate services, and develop teacher education programs.

Although these laws for the most part have fostered and improved the education of exceptional students, they have also had their share of critics. Many parents and educators believe that integration is not necessarily the key to educational success and that such popular practices as mainstreaming and inclusion are not always in the best interests of exceptional students.

Controversies

Notwithstanding the gratuitous claim that no child be left behind, research clearly shows this not to be the case. The No Child Left Behind (NCLB) Act has created serious problems for school districts and their special education students in the area of assessment and testing. Under NCLB, all schools are required to report "adequate yearly progress," which is measured by standardized testing. The results of these tests are used by the national government to determine whether or not schools are succeeding. Schools with low test scores are labeled as failing schools. Special education students and English language learners must take the same standardized tests as their non-disabled peers. For the most part, success in this endeavor is unrealistic and in many cases simply unfair. Despite this, their scores are counted, and are often responsible for lowering a school's success rate. The groups who do poorly are often targeted and directly blamed for a school's failure. The response by state and local communities and school districts to this issue has become so strong that the national government is exploring alternative means of assessment for diverse students. This process has not yet been determined.

Despite legal mandates, implementations of mainstreaming, inclusion, and other innovative educational practices, critics outline numerous serious problems. Because much of the legislation has been implemented based on theoretical beliefs and not actual data results, it is not clear whether or not the process of integration works positively for most exceptional students. Though appropriate programs appear to have been put in place, there are still far too many children whose needs have not been met, who are falling through the cracks. The legislation to assist these students has moved faster than most educators' abilities to fulfill it. Mainstream children, teachers, and parents are poorly or rarely even prepared to understand and interact with exceptional children. For these and countless other reasons, students are still being placed in inappropriate classroom settings with teachers unqualified to meet their needs. They are not receiving needed resources, services, and materials. Children continue to be misclassified and mislabeled, and suffer the many detrimental side effects of such actions. Although many educators and parents believe special classes better serve their children, some parents are determined to see their children find success, support, and friendship in public school settings. Parents remain their children's most effective advocates. Learning to navigate the system brings unexpected rewards not only for their children, but for all children (Belkin, 2004). As you continue to observe in classrooms, see if any of these issues catch your eye. Consider the following questions:

For whom are special classes appropriate? What might be some positive and negative aspects of labeling? What are mainstreaming and inclusion? How should general education teachers, students, and parents be prepared for the practices of mainstreaming and inclusion? What questions do you have as a prospective teacher?

The Multicultural Circle

Autobiography can again become the focal point when a multicultural circle is formed to explore issues of diversity. The participants of the circle describe incidents in which they were "labeled" by others. This sharing helps them to see the ways in which we all endure identity issues and makes everyone more aware of the need to address such critical themes in the classroom. Krasnow and Schlechter (in Sobelman, 1999) present a vivid picture of their experiences in enacting the multicultural circle with their classes:

Its goal is to have the students learn more deeply about diversity by exploring each other's identities through the telling of individual stories. Often moving and intimate, this activity takes place at about the mid-point in the semester after a strong feeling of community and trust has been established. How this activity proceeds in class is dependent upon the instructors. One version of the multicultural circle is for everyone in the class to sit in a circle with the invitation to tell a story about the self that illustrates one or several of the identity categories we have been discussing in class. Another version uses five or six students and an instructor sitting in a fishbowl around the larger class. Either format produces powerful and personal stories for everyone to hear. The multicultural circle tends to emphasize the unique in each person's life history. Gradually with the telling of enough stories, students begin to hear the similarities as well as differences that connect us.

Since many prospective teachers will be teaching in areas with significantly diverse populations, they must clearly understand and acknowledge their own belief systems before they can work sensitively with others unlike themselves. After all our years of teaching this course we consider the interaction among autobiography, the beliefs students have developed, and the new found awareness of talking across and through differences to be a pinnacle achievement for each section each term. (p. 40)

The multicultural circle dramatizes rich and often raw, unforgettable slices of real life and helps its participants internalize the pains and joys of who we all are. Students bring forth countless stories of how the labels assigned to them influenced their sense of self. Though profound in its personal affect, this activity also brings to the surface the multiple themes and challenges we have raised in this chapter.

Talking about diversity is a daunting task for any teacher and a disturbing experience for many students. In many cases, students are resistant and unwilling to talk about these issues in the presence of their peers. Some students get angry; some are offended; some are simply afraid to speak. Despite these reactions, educators must fight complacency and deliberately provoke and promote respectful discussion. The silences must be broken. Teachers and students must talk face-to-face and heart-to-heart to learn about what binds and separates individuals from one another. Timing is everything and such activity cannot take place in a vacuum. Like teaching any other subject, careful scaffolding and preparation must be in place, including the creation of a secure environment in which a classroom community has already been established.

Having explored the powerful effects of naming and labeling, we hope you have new lenses with which to view life in classrooms, schools, and communities. As our world grows smaller, the need to understand each other grows greater. Learning to talk about diversity in its many manifestations, as difficult as it may be, offers all of us a richer and deeper appreciation of who we all are.

Describe an incident in your life that "slapped you in the face" and unexpectedly gave your identity a label. How did it make you feel? Can you remember instances when you labeled others?

Teachers and Teaching

A Teacher's Poem

I am a New York City public high school teacher
Do not look surprised.
Do not feel sorry for me.
Do not pity me.
Do not offer me your condolences.
Do not pat me on the back, shake my hand,
Cross yourself or speak of my bravery.
Do not ask me if I receive combat pay
Or wear a bulletproof vest.
Do not ask me when I plan to get a real job,
Apply to law school,
Or what my first career choice was.
Do not assume my head is in the clouds
And I have no grasp on reality.
Do not sympathize, empathize,
Or tell me about the job opening in your cousin's business.
Do not suggest I join the Peace Corps.
Do not ask if my parents were teachers.
Do not ask if my parents were hippies.
Do not assume I am a saint, naïve, innocent,
Searching for my childhood,
Living for the summers off,
Home by 2:15,
Use a red pen,

Play the Lotto,
Wish for the glory days of the past
Or would rather work in the suburbs where I could *really* teach.
I am a New York City public high school teacher
Ask me why I chose to be a teacher.
Ask me if my students have books, supplies and chairs.
Ask me my opinion of Giuliani, Pataki and Crew.
Reminisce with me about your favorite teachers,
Share with me the qualities that made them admirable.
Tell me about your favorite projects and field trips.
Ask me what my students are working on now.
Gasp when I say how many students are in each of my classes
Gasp when I say how many I see in a week.
Cry with me about Marc sleeping in the subway,
Simone losing her father,
Maria thinking she is pregnant,
And Rick dropping out of school.
Laugh with me about Kenny (caught in the act) insisting it was the "Stalin in him,"
My classroom being toilet papered,
And the Great All-Out Classroom Trash Throwing War of '94
(fought just to get Sharon to smile on the last day of school).
Marvel with me over my students' intelligence
Achievements, diligence, creativity and strength.
Cheer with me as they write their college essays and take their SATs.
Soar with me as they get their college acceptance letters.
Ask me how to create a scholarship,
Ask me how to volunteer,
Ask me about the many qualities needed to become
A New York City public high school teacher.

By Lisa Lauritzen

Originally published in The New York Times, September 9, 1997.

(Guiliani, Pataki, and Crew refer to the Mayor of New York City, the Governor of New York State, and the New York City Schools' Chancellor at the time the poem was written.)

Lisa Lauritzen's poem and our experiences contradict much of the criticism that is directed at teachers. Most of the classroom teachers with whom we have worked are very special people who go unrecognized and unappreciated. Too often they work under difficult conditions. Too often they are applauded only on designated "teacher recognition" days. Too often they are abused in the media. In too many communities they are underpaid and held to unreasonable expectations. Parker J. Palmer writes of the "courage to teach" (1998) and Joseph McDonald describes teaching as an "uncertain craft" (1992). John Mayher (1990) wants teachers to have "uncommon sense," and Vito Perrone (1999) calls for teachers with "passion." We tend to cite the accounts of the great teachers as exceptions to the majority—from Jesus to Socrates to Dewey—to the one whose memory you hold dear, but there are many caring, creative, dedicated, and effective teachers to whom we can turn as inspirational models. To benefit most from what they have taught us about teaching and learning, we need to situate them in time and place, to see both the sources of their commitments and the constraints that they struggled against. We need to study them carefully so that we can build upon their strengths and learn from their limitations.

Autobiography Again

We return to the concept of autobiography because, as Britzman (1991) claims, "it is not just the university that fashions the student teacher's pedagogy; the student teacher's life history, both in and out of classrooms, offers definitions of what it means to learn and to teach" (p. 47).

It is not uncommon to find that prospective teachers depend on the memories of their teachers as they begin to develop their own persona. Dan Lortie (1975) refers to this as the "apprenticeship of observation," leading prospective teachers to enact the "teach as I was taught" principle. While some of you may attribute your choice of a teaching career to the inspiration of former teachers and aim to model yourself after them, others of you may reject the models your teachers offered and may want to be very different from them.

In *Lessons for New Teachers,* Perrone (1990) probes key underlying principles and practices of mindful teaching and learning. He insists, "Teachers need a powerful philosophical base, a compass to guide them in their ongoing work" (p. 52). In our words, your philosophy should be mirrored in your practice. It not only includes beliefs set forth by renowned educators, but also your experiences, attitudes, and beliefs about the world around you. Curriculum content must be embedded in moral purposes and in learners' lives. Too often students ask their teachers, "Why do we need to learn this?" When teachers transform scripted lessons into active inquiries, their philosophical bases will inform how students perceive and understand knowledge. The students will no longer need to ask that question.

Perrone (1990) also asserts that teachers should be able to identify and articulate their own "intellectual passions" (p. 63). When teachers can convey what they care most about, their students will sense and share that passion. By connecting the events in the classroom with the outside world, students and their teachers link intellectual pursuits to real life issues. The combination of a teacher's philosophical bases and intellectual passion fuels the power for exciting teaching and learning.

Describe your most favorite or least favorite teacher. Why do you feel as you do about this individual? What do you think were your teacher's philosophical beliefs and passions about teaching and learning, and how were they enacted in the classroom? How do you think your teacher influenced your decision to become a teacher and to define the role you see for yourself?

If you share your teacher stories with your peers or colleagues, you may find that perceptions of effective teachers vary greatly as much for their style as their attitude. Some teach by example, others by performing. Some capture students' attention by the manner in which they present knowledge; others provoke and challenge students to seek out the knowledge. Some exert tight control in the classroom; others invite negotiation. Some seek to know a great deal about their students while others tend to remain remote from students' personal lives. In any case, it is critical to remember the important roles a teacher played in your life.

Anyone Can Teach . . . That's What YOU Think!

Sharon Feiman-Nemser and Margret Buchman (1985) explain that because we all went to school, many people believe that anyone can teach. They see this as a negative perception lessening the appreciation of teaching as a challenging profession. David Larabee (2005) suggests that teaching looks deceptively simple when viewed from the little seats in the classroom. "It looks like a set of routines, a process of maintaining order, a matter of nature and personality. Invisible is all the planning, decision making, moment-to-moment adjustment to student actions, and professional reflection." (p. 189)

As Lisa Lauritzen so vividly conveys in "A Teacher's Poem," teaching is not easy, but it can be satisfying and rewarding. Each of the teachers we introduce you to underscores the challenge and the gratification of teaching; each of them also shows the power of good theories, the value of ongoing reflection, and the need to reject the public's negative and often uninformed perceptions. Each of the stories demonstrates a teacher's unique talent to raise the level of teaching far beyond minimal standards.

We invite you to form a book group with your peers or colleagues to share your responses to one or more of the teacher autobiographies listed below. If you are unable to talk with colleagues, choose among the texts we describe and use the questions we pose to begin your independent exploration.

Berger, Ron. (2003). An Ethic of Excellence: Building a Culture of Craftsmanship with Students. Portsmouth: Heinemann.

Drawing from his own experience as a teacher and a craftsman, Berger gives us a vision of educational reform that transcends standards, curriculum, and instructional strategies. He shares many of his instructional approaches as he makes his case for a paradigm shift to an "ethic of excellence."

How would you define Berger's philosophy of teaching and learning? What counts as evidence of Berger's success? Where do teaching and craftsmanship come together?

Codell, Esme Raji. (1999). Educating Esme: Diary of a Teacher's First Year. Chapel Hill: Algonquin Books.

Codell's diary is about the life of a first-year teacher. She has come to an inner-city Chicago elementary school to teach—and she's not going to let incompetent administrators, abusive parents, gang members, weary teachers, angry children, or her own insecurities get in the way. She is fresh mouthed yet compassionate; she can be stubborn and generous, cynical and charming. In this record of her frustrations, her achievements, and her struggles to maintain her individuality in the face of bureaucracy, she reveals what it takes to be a genuine teacher.

As a new teacher, how did Codell manage to maintain her beliefs and enthusiasm in a school with a conflicting philosophy? How realistic were Codell's expectations for herself and her students?

Greeley, Kathy. (2000). "Why Fly That Way?" Linking Community and Academic Achievement. NY: Teachers College Press.

In the Foreword to Greeley's account, Deborah Meier writes: "Any time we practice our craft without first building bonds between learners, we do grave personal injury to many of our students and simultaneously fail to teach most of them well." This is the story of a middle school teacher who struggles to create a classroom community with the result that she enhances the self-esteem and the academic achievement of the students in her "class from hell."

How do the school and community contexts support Greeley and her students? To what extent is mindful learning achieved in Greeley's class? How does Greeley's flexible use of time reveal her beliefs about teaching and learning?

Logan, Judy. (1993) Teaching Stories. NY: Kodansha/Oxford Press.

Logan's stories show that she is a teacher committed to gender equity and multiculturalism. Herbert Kohl wrote: "Judy Logan's book is an intimate and moving look at the lives of children who have often been neglected, marginalized, or excluded in the schools. It reveals the ways in which a compassionate and caring educator can help children overcome the foolishness and damage done by systems that stigmatize instead of educate children. It is a telling of tales—a recounting of stories that make it difficult to forget or ignore the needs of all children and the ways in which caring adults can and do make a difference."

Was Logan too personally involved with her students and their families? Do you agree or disagree with Logan's principle that a teacher should never say "no" to a student's ideas? What gender issues does this book raise?

Michie, Gregory. (1999). Holler If You Hear Me: The Education of a Teacher and His Students. NY: Teachers College Press.

Weaving back and forth between Gregory Michie's awakening as a teacher and the first-person stories of his students, Holler If You Hear Me creates an intimate and compassionate portrayal of what it means to be a teacher and a student in urban America. While not shying away from hard truths, Michie lends a measure of hope, humor, and practical insight about the difficult work of teaching for social justice. In the process, he brings us the stories of his students both in his words and theirs, giving voice to Latino and African-American youth who often go unheard.

> *What lessons does Michie learn about himself and his students? Where did Michie eventually determine the blame should be placed for the problems he was having in his classroom? What personal and professional beliefs guided Michie in reaching, understanding, and teaching his students?*

Paley, Vivian Gussin. (1992). You Can't Say You Can't Play. Cambridge: Harvard University Press.

Vivian Paley, a MacArthur prize-winning educator, takes a fascinating look at the moral dimensions of the classroom. She introduces a new rule to her kindergarten students: "you can't say you can't play." The struggle that ensues presents a great teacher with her greatest challenge. In her account of the social relations among children, Paley explores how to keep children from being ignored by their classmates and illustrates how the teacher's art can attack the evil of exclusion at its childhood roots.

> *Can you recall a time when you felt that you were being "left out"? Would you have wanted someone to intervene on your behalf? How would you respond to the criticism that Paley's rule is not always appropriate or democratic? How might teachers and students negotiate the rules for their classroom?*

Although the teacher narratives we have chosen tend to emphasize the caring relationships that form between teachers and their students, they also illustrate how teachers organize subject knowledge to engage their students in learning. By creating the balance between the affective and the cognitive they make their classrooms personally meaningful and intellectually challenging.

Regrettably, many teachers face obstacles that defeat their best intentions. The research conducted by Linda McNeil (1986) exposes the "contradictions of control" to which teachers are frequently subjected within their schools' structures. Many teachers report that they are working in environments that inhibit their developing the curricula they believe their students need. These teachers, many of whom are talented experts in their field, are fully qualified to be curriculum decision makers. Instead they find themselves hampered by texts that fail to arrive, by the mandate to implement scripted, "teacher-proof" materials, and by "the tension between the administrative purposes and the instructional purposes of the school" (p. 68). These contradictions seriously undermine the soul of the profession and lead to what McNeil describes as "de-skilling" teachers (p. 76).

> *During your various experiences in schools and classrooms, try to note any*
> *controlling indicators you see and think about how they impact on teaching and*
> *learning. Also, try to find examples where teachers struggle to maneuver around the*
> *constraints imposed upon them. What strategies might you employ to cope with*
> *these kinds of problems?*

Fortunately, not all teachers succumb to the impositions McNeil found, and many are able to creatively blaze successful paths that meet both students' and administrators' needs. What we hope you noted is that the teachers' memoirs highlight qualities beyond the technical model. They illuminate teachers as active learners, caring human beings, risk-takers, and social activists.

In this chapter, although we do not underestimate the importance of the technical aspects of teaching—formulating objectives, planning lessons, managing the classroom, developing a repertoire of instructional strategies, and employing assessment and evaluation procedures—we do not dwell on them. Although these components of teaching are critically important, our goal is to draw your attention to aspects of teachers and teaching that often go unmentioned.

Metaphors for Teachers and Teaching

In *Metaphors We Live By* (1980, 2003) George Lakoff and Mark Johnson, a linguist and a philosopher, respectively, explain that the metaphors we commonly employ in our everyday language not only enhance the effectiveness of our communication, but more significantly structure our perceptions and reveal how we think about important aspects of our lives. Lakoff and Johnson claim that "metaphor is pervasive in everyday life" and that "our ordinary conceptual system, in terms of which we both think and act, is fundamentally metaphoric in nature." In showing that our thought processes are metaphorical, they offer us a new way to examine how our words reveal what we are thinking.

Metaphors frequently appear in our conversations as well as in the texts we read about teachers and teaching. As we listen to the language teachers and laypersons use, we discover that they are drawing on a lexicon associated with fields as diverse as medicine, law, corporate management, psychology, agriculture, war, and sports. If we pay careful attention to their language we can see attitudes and assumptions that impact on the expectations people hold for teachers' roles and behaviors.

What concepts of teaching lie behind terms such as "counselor" "drill sergeant," "friend," "enforcer," "mentor," "diagnostician," "judge," and "warrior"? What might be the differences between those who say teaching is "exploring" or "coaching" or "planting seeds" as compared with others who use the words "informing" or "managing" or "policing"? What do you think Lisa Lauritzen's metaphors might be? What are yours?

In the same way that we urged you to critically examine how your timeline and vignette depict your learning experiences, we urge to write about your image of yourself as teacher. In addition, think about your description of your favorite teacher and the memoirs written by practicing teachers. What metaphors can you identify? By taking a second look, can you see how metaphors help to reveal an individual's perspective on teaching?

When you apply for a teaching position, you may decide to develop a teaching portfolio that documents your studies and your work. Included in that portfolio should be your "pedagogic creed" (a la Dewey, 1897), a statement that explains your beliefs about education and your goals as a teacher. Undoubtedly, you will revise your statement several times, but start now with an early draft. Identify the metaphors you employ and consider their implications for how you are presenting yourself and your educational philosophy.

Teachers as Collaborators

Collaboration among teachers occurs in a variety of settings. Teachers who are teaching the same grade or course to different groups of students may choose to plan together. In other schools, clusters of teachers of different subjects meet to decide how to integrate their areas with a common theme. Specialist teachers who work with many different classes try to relate their specialty to the overall curriculum by meeting periodically with the classroom teacher.

Probably the most challenging, and we would claim, most satisfying form of collaboration is team teaching. In the most common team teaching format, two teachers jointly design and enact unit and lesson plans. The team members may be teachers of the same grade or the same content area or they may represent different disciplines. In inclusion classrooms, special education teachers work side-by-side with their general education counterparts.

A key aspect of collaboration requires that teachers negotiate their individual roles in the classroom. In one model, they interact in front of the class, offering different perspectives; in another model, they take turns leading the class; in a third model, they work with different groups within the class. They may share or divide responsibilities for recordkeeping, responding to students' work, and grading. When meeting and planning, they share their observations of students' progress, and reflect on their own processes and how they might be improved.

Team teaching gives students the opportunity to relate to two personalities and gives teachers the benefit of another person's expertise, perspective, insights, and feedback. It demands that teachers be willing to take risks, develop a trusting relationship with a colleague, and ensure that tasks are divided equally. Team teaching is not for everyone. We have learned that it is most successful when teachers choose to team teach and have some choice in their partner.

Teachers as Change Agents

Hollywood has contributed, probably unintentionally, to the idealized images students, parents, and policymakers have of teachers. Contrary to the real world of many teachers, the films show highly romanticized versions of teaching. Yet, among a considerably uneven collection, a select few raise viewers' consciousness about teachers, teachers who choose the road less traveled, who advocate for their students, who change the life of a child, who create dynamic classrooms, who impact on the life of a school and community, and even teachers whose own lives are changed as a result of their teaching. Included among the available videos are several that we have found particularly effective: *Children of a Lesser God* (1986), *Conrack* (1997), *Mr. Holland's Opus* (1996), *Music of the Heart* (1999), *Searching for Bobby Fisher* (1993), and *Stand and Deliver* (1988). In Appendix B, Teaching and Learning Hollywood Style, we offer a longer but not exhaustive list of available videos.

The teachers portrayed in these movies, as well as in the autobiographies you have read, can be described as change agents. When viewed from that position these protagonists expand our conception of a teacher from one who tries to satisfy and reproduce the status quo to one who actively works at meeting the needs of students, critiquing and redefining the curriculum, and changing structures and relationships within and beyond the school. Most importantly, these teachers grow personally, learning about themselves from their students, colleagues, and their own actions and reactions to the situations around them. To be a change agent is to have overarching peripheral vision.

Teacher agency was the focus of Cynthia Paris's research (1993) of four elementary school teachers who were expected to integrate the use of computers into their classrooms. To establish a framework for her investigation, Paris defines teacher agency in terms of curriculum change:

The term agency assumes not only a particular role for teachers that is at variance with prevailing assumptions of the teacher as technician or as implementer of others' ideas, but also a conception of curriculum not as a reified and easily generalizable commodity, but as an evolving, context-specific interaction between teachers, children, and content. (p. 16)

Paris found that all four of the teachers she studied became active agents of change, but each one used her autonomy to approach and to solve the problem differently.

Michael Fullan has been studying the complexities of the change process in educational organizations for many years. In *Change Forces: Probing the Depths of Educational Reform* (1993), he expands Paris's conception of teacher agency by identifying four capacities of the teacher as change agent: personal vision-building, inquiry, mastery, and collaboration. He writes convincingly that the individual teacher "is a critical starting point because the leverage for change can be far greater through the efforts of individuals, and each educator has more control (more than is exercised) over what he or she does, because it is one's own motives and skills that are at question." Fullan reassures teachers that they "do not have to wallow in hubris in realizing that they are in a strategic position." But, on the other hand, he challenges them toward "pursuing moral purpose with greater and greater skill, conceptualizing their roles on a higher plane than they currently do" (pp. 12–13). For Fullan, change agency and moral purpose are closely allied:

We need to go public with a new rationale for why teaching and teacher development is so fundamental to the future of society. We need to begin to practice on a wide scale what is implicit in the moral purpose of teaching. To do so we need the capacities of change agency. (p. 18)

Moral purpose takes on a political dimension for Peter McLaren (1989), who, along with Paolo Friere, Michael Apple, and Henry Giroux are among the best known advocates of a critical pedagogy. According to McLaren, for these educators, teacher agency is conceived in radical terms:

Critical educational theorists argue that teachers must understand the role that schooling plays in joining knowledge and power, in order to use that role for the development of critical and active citizens. The traditional view of classroom instruction and learning as a neutral process antiseptically removed from the concepts of power, politics, history, and context can no longer be credibly endorsed. (p. 160)

Teacher agency in its moral or political proportions may seem to be an unreasonable expectation to set for the beginning teacher. Yet, it is quite evident that the teachers who find genuine satisfaction in their work are the ones who make commitments to redefining their roles and changing their expectations for teaching and learning. As you contemplate the qualities you hope will define you as a teacher, you may want to reflect upon how you wish to be perceived, and how you will go about becoming that person. That choice is yours. The opportunities are there for you to define yourself as broadly as you can at this time, but to realize that as you gain increased expertise you can take on new professional goals.

Teachers as Reflective Practitioners

Responding to the many questions we have been posing demands much serious thought on the part of the prospective teacher. We would like to assume that many of you find yourselves examining some of your assumptions, and deconstructing and reconstructing various schooling experiences to gain new insights about education and its many controversies. Learning to develop and hone such skills is critical to your continuing development as a teacher and learner because you must always be working to uncover the deep structures behind your thoughts and actions, as well as those of your students. These actions will facilitate your becoming a reflective practitioner, asking *your* questions and working to explain *your* thinking and experiences.

Reflective practice is identified with professionals in a range of fields who engage in what Donald Schön (1983) calls "reflection in action." These professionals are careful and routine observers, sensitive and attentive to the dynamics of their environment. Their alertness enables them to make immediate decisions that often change the direction of their work. Reflective teachers are responsive to the happenings that occur in their classrooms. They can modify or redirect their plans to meet or create teachable moments. In your case, as preservice teachers, reflection takes on somewhat different dimensions. You may or may not yet be in a position where you can modify curriculum or instruction, but you should reflect on the actions you see. Think about your beliefs and about the ideas you are encountering as a student and observer.

At the most concrete level, reflection evolves from the notion of a mirror whose "bending back" produces an image. This leads the viewer to ask: How do I see myself? Why do I see myself as I do? What might I want to change about the image I see? At a more abstract level, reflection involves thinking about thinking. This kind of reflection is often referred to as *metacognition*. The fundamental questions now become: What do I know? How do I know what I know? What are the implications of what I know? What more do I need to know? To answer these questions requires that you be persistent, curious, and flexible as you draw on prior knowledge and seek out alternative perspectives. Because writing is a means of thinking—reflection is often best enacted when you record your thoughts—look back at what you have written and maintain openness to interpreting, modifying, and adapting your ideas.

Bending back to study one's mirror image, deliberating about one's ideas and experiences, and searching for deeper insights into one's thinking are essential aspects of the reflective repertoire. As you become increasingly adept at this kind of thinking, you will be preparing yourself with the strategies to reflect when you are in your own classroom as a teacher. Reflection should also help you synthesize the many beliefs and ideas you have been examining. The early synthesis should then lead you toward articulating your personal philosophy of education, a dynamic philosophy that you refine throughout your career.

Teachers as Researchers

Any teacher with a sense of uncertainty is a teacher-researcher. You can be a questioner for whom classroom problems become issues to investigate, a learner seeking to better understand one's self and one's students, or an observer looking over and over again to uncover the mysteries within your classroom. Action-oriented teacher research has several features that distinguishes it from other types of research:

- Teachers are central both as the investigators and as the audience.
- Context cannot be separated from what is under study.
- The researcher is an integral part of the study and does not stand apart from what he or she is studying.
- The research is most likely to focus on immediate and practical events of daily school life.
- The results of the research contribute most directly to both the teachers' and learners' development in that specific research context. However, the results may affect other classrooms as well.

The writings of several scholars (Burnaford, Fischer, & Hobson, 2001; Cochran-Smith & Lytle, 1993; Goswami & Stillman, 1987; Stenhouse, 1975) significantly influenced the movement to encourage teachers to be researchers. The primary goal is well stated in the title, *Becoming Our Own Experts,* a book produced by a group of British teachers (Talk Workshop Group, 1982).

Though some people argue that teacher research makes an additional and unfair demand on teachers, others insist that teacher research is a means of empowering and professionalizing teachers. Furthermore, proponents claim that research reduces the loneliness and sense of helplessness of classroom teachers. They can collaborate with their students and create joint efforts that enhance communication and teaching and learning. Collegial collaboration can lead to mutual support and strengthen cooperation among members of a school faculty. Networks available through the Internet enable teachers to expand their professional interactions by reaching out to colleagues across time and space.

In the next chapter, you will be introduced to some of the basic methods of qualitative educational research. Most particularly, you will learn how to observe, record, analyze, and interpret findings. Such skills will enable you to become teacher-researchers who can study your classrooms, identify instructional problems, and systematically set about addressing them. To ensure that you continue to refine these skills, we suggest that you seek opportunities to be a teacher-researcher even while you are still a prospective teacher.

Metaphors aside, the multifaceted role of teacher is intensely demanding and time consuming, far surpassing the 9-to-3 schedule that many perceive it to be. It's not for the passive or the timid, but rather for those who are willing to take the time and responsibility to strengthen themselves and thereby contribute to an educational system that respects their professionalism.

Perhaps the last word belongs to Susan Ohanian (1999):

> . . . the best thing a teacher has to offer is herself. . . . It means that in the end we have no plans, no theories, no checklists to hide behind. . . . After we read everything we can get our hands on, after we study and travel to conferences, and work hard to become smart in our profession, the best moments in our classroom come from impulse, not from carefully constructed plans. This is why I am skeptical about national teaching standards: How do you test for a sense of humor? A good heart? A generous spirit? A tolerance for ambiguity? An ability to step in at the right moment as well as the ability to step back and take the long pause? Standardistos seem to tell us that competence is enough. Garrison Keillor observes, "Love brings people to safety when competence can go no further." Where is the test for love? (p. 56)

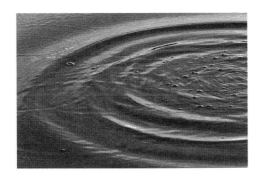

CHAPTER 6

Observing Teaching and Learning

In the preceding chapter, we tried to make the case that teachers who become researchers systematically examine their teaching and their students' learning. For inservice teachers, classroom observation is more accessible but often more difficult to manage. Yet, when teachers can sit back and observe the actions, interactions, and activities in which their students are engaged, they are often surprised by what they see. Their discoveries frequently lead them to revising assignments, clarifying directions, restructuring time, and attending to individual students whose needs had gone unrecognized.

The circumstances are quite different for preservice teachers. Until recently, most students in teacher preparation programs had few opportunities to study what happens in classrooms. Their curricula culminated with a short semester of student teaching, followed in most cases by graduation and a search for their first teaching position. They quickly discovered that their time in the field was far too short for them to absorb all the realities and responsibilities that teaching demands. Teacher educators concurred. In order to address these crucial omissions, today's programs are likely to embed field experience throughout the students' course of study, providing opportunities for them to observe and participate in a range of community, school, and nonformal educational settings.

When most prospective teachers begin their professional studies they tend to view being a teacher from the perspective of life as a student. Early observations in educational settings lead them to shed the "student only" vantage point and expand their awareness of the many contexts where teaching and learning occur. In his landmark study, *Life in Classrooms* (1968), Philip W. Jackson writes:

> *Classroom life . . . is too complex an affair to be viewed or talked about from a single perspective. . . . Accordingly, as we try to grasp the meaning of what school is like for students and teachers we must not hesitate to use all the ways of knowing at*

our disposal. This means we must read, and look, and listen, and count things, and talk to people, and even muse introspectively over the memories of our childhood. (p. viii)

Jackson opens the door for you to step inside a classroom and take an holistic look, discovering facets, activities, and interactions that you might not notice otherwise. His invitation applies equally to looking at how teaching and learning occur in nonformal settings beyond the school building. By also observing in environments such as museums, parks, botanical gardens, and acquaria, future teachers can expand their purview to include how professionals working outside the formal contexts for schooling enhance students' knowledge about the physical, artistic, and natural worlds.

Becoming Mindful Observers

To build an early bridge between theory and practice, observation places the prospective teacher in educational surroundings to begin inquiring into the real world of teaching and learning. This type of inquiry requires an understanding of the role observation plays and the ability to use a variety of observation strategies. In this chapter we outline how to look in order to see, how to capture a picture, and how to stand close and away. Our goal is to prepare you to be a skilled observer so that, with a careful eye and an open mind, what may appear as ordinary events will lead you to new insights about what teachers and learners do in different situations. Here we provide the schema for you to become an active observer and to engage in the process of creating a teaching-learning portrait. Although in the sections that follow we continue to refer to teachers, learners, and classrooms, we intend these words to apply as well to educators, students, and settings in locations both within and beyond traditional school walls.

By creating a teaching-learning portrait, one can capture and interpret significant aspects of classroom life. "The challenge we face as educators is to explore an ethnographic stance as a habit of mind, not just a special project " (Short et al., 2004). Drawing from the work of Sara Lightfoot (1983) we have adopted the term *portrait* to suggest that for any description or picture that you create you will be doing what many artists do. "Portraitists seek to record and interpret the perspectives and experiences of the people they are studying, documenting their voices and their visions—their authority, knowledge, and wisdom" (Lawrence-Lightfoot & Davis, 1997, p. xv). As you draw on the details of what you see and hear over time, as well as on your impressions of that situation, we hope you will discover a great deal about the classroom experience from the perspectives of both students and their teachers.

It should be relatively easy to identify students' and teachers' physical characteristics. The real challenge is to get beneath these surface features to learn about the implicit as well as the explicit aspects of the educational environment. Through repeated contacts in the field, an observer is able to pursue various avenues, challenge preconceived notions, reexamine early impressions, and avoid forming unfounded conclusions. William Ayers (1993) reminds us:

We must find a way, too, to ground our observations in many dimensions at once: intellectual, cultural, physical, spiritual, emotional. . . .We must try to see beyond our own stereotypes and prejudices, beyond some notion of how children ought to behave. . . .We must see beyond the unstated assumption driving most schools, the wacky idea that children [and adolescents] are puny, inadequate adults and that the job of education is to transport them as quickly as possible from that sorry state. We must look unblinkingly at the way [they] are, and struggle to make sense of everything that we see in order to teach them. (p. 33)

At the same time, we must learn to look at teachers from many angles, striving to understand their beliefs, goals, concerns, styles, and instructional decisions. In a chapter entitled "Approaches to Teaching" (pp. 71–93), Perrone (1999) describes aspects of teaching that you might look for during your observations. His suggestions include looking at: beginnings and endings, expectations, administrative tasks, student engagements, the use of language, the posing of questions, materials, discussions, and small-group processes.

Alfie Kohn (1999) provides another excellent and interesting source for looking at classrooms. He brings to light aspects of schooling so familiar one might forget to look for them. These include school furniture arrangements, wall content and décor in classrooms and halls, faces and voices of teachers, staff and children, the kinds of sounds and silences emanating from classrooms, the location of teachers during instruction, and other significant "stuff" found within the classroom. Though intended to assist parents in choosing classrooms for their children, his visitor's guide (pp. 236–237) can assist observers as well. As professionals, we must continually learn to see ourselves not only as teachers, but also as observers and researchers.

Students and teachers constantly engage in observation to learn about and participate in their worlds, but seldom consider what guides their observations. An ethnographic perspective provides a lens for identifying and examining the cultural patterns and practices of life within classrooms and communities. While teachers and students have traditionally been seen as consumers of knowledge produced by others, they can use inquiry to construct knowledge and to critique their world by becoming researchers. (Short et al., 2004, p. 367)

Field Notes

Field notes are the observers' ongoing, written accounts of what they hear, see, experience, feel, and think about in the course of observations. It is the place to record the details as objectively as possible, "to capture a word-picture" of the learners and teacher(s) in their setting. These notes serve to document the conclusions present in the portrait.

It is essential that you record the information gathered at several observation sessions. We suggest that you not take notes while observing or conversing. Note-taking interferes with your attending to what you are seeing and hearing and also is distracting and discomforting to those being observed.

Immediately after each observation you should take a few minutes to jot down in words, and possibly drawings, what you observed. The most difficult part of this task is to separate what you saw from what you think it meant. You might want to divide your page in half, using one side to describe exactly what you saw and the other side to interpret what you saw. In all likelihood, no matter how good a memory you have, you will lose some of the details; repeated observations, however, should ensure that over time you will become a more competent note-taker and will retain what is most relevant. When you have more time, you should write an extended entry for that day, elaborating and reflecting upon your experience and identifying the questions that emerged for you.

Does This Place Look Familiar?

Many of you may find this undertaking places you for the first time as an observer rather than as a student. In your timeline and vignette you may have already identified one or more of your most meaningful early learning experiences, but as you enter a classroom as an observer, be prepared for more flashes of memory. Inevitably, you will bring with you expectations based on your own schooling, leading to judgments about the students and teachers you see based on your own likes and dislikes and your own successes or disappointments. None of us can, or should, attempt to erase our recollections, but if we are to expand our understandings of "life in classrooms" today, we must guard against making new assumptions based upon those memories. We must be sensitive to the fact that every classroom in every school, grade, and subject is different, even when taught by the same teacher. What might seem all too familiar is really not familiar at all.

Margot Ely (1991) describes the delicate balance an observer must maintain.

In opposition to what many budding ethnography students believe, observation will never be objective and . . . will never be judgment-free. This is so because observation comes out of what the observer selects to see and chooses to note. All we can work for is that our vision is not too skewed by our own subjectivities. And that means work for most of us. . . . The process entails becoming increasingly more aware of our own "eyeglasses," our own blinders, so that these do not color unfairly both what we observe and what we detail in writing. (pp. 53–54)

Prepare for Your Observations

The first step is identifying the setting or classroom you wish to observe. As a prospective observer you must negotiate when the observations will take place. Other matters to be negotiated might include obtaining a list of the names of the students, gaining access to students' work, obtaining information about the curriculum and materials being used, and scheduling meetings with the teacher. Because classrooms do not exist in a vacuum, it is also helpful to learn about the school's policies, calendar, schedule, routines, procedures, expectations, and curriculum.

Before entering the classroom, you should think about how you would like to introduce yourself, and should opportunities arise, what questions you might pose to the teacher or students. We also suggest that you review Perrone's and Kohn's vantage points regarding what to look for as you observe.

Finally, there are common courtesies that you should maintain:

- Come on time and remain for the entire class period. Teaching is often unpredictable and one can never be too surprised by the unanticipated and unexpected.
- Avoid interrupting the ongoing activity and resist the temptation to chat with the students and teacher during this time.
- If you are invited to join a discussion or participate in a small group, be guided by the teacher's expectations.
- Be aware of the fine line between observation and participation. Do not attempt to introduce your agenda or dominate a conversation.

Portraying Teaching and Learning

You will need to be flexible and able to adapt in whatever setting you are conducting your observations. In an elementary school, you probably will focus on the events in a single classroom. If you are observing in a secondary school, you might find that the teacher moves from one class to another. In either situation, you should make every attempt to observe the teacher and the students in multiple settings—the classroom, office, lunchroom, hallway—as a whole class, in small groups, as individuals, and on field trips. Nonschool settings might require a little more creativity and responsiveness to the specific environment as you observe.

As you focus on concrete examples of actual teaching and learning, the observations should help you begin to connect theory to practice, to parallel what you have been reading with what you are seeing. You should begin to recognize the diversity and individuality of students, teachers, and classrooms. As an observer, you may find your initial perceptions challenged, confirmed, revised, or confused, but conversations with your peers can provide opportunities for both unraveling and revisioning your ongoing experiences. Exploratory talk that analyzes and evaluates the numerous dimensions of your observations should help you work through your initial dilemmas, questions, concerns, and beliefs.

We stated at the beginning of this chapter that field experiences serve to facilitate the transition from student-learner to teacher-learner. We also acknowledged that your personal views of schooling should not be forgotten. Having said this does not imply that a portrait is an impressionistic presentation. Quite to the contrary. Because you are engaging in an actual form of ethnographic research, your portrait should emerge from the observational data you have gleaned and recorded.

As you prepare to write your portrait, you will need strategies for organizing your data. The first step is to reread your field notes sequentially to get an overview of what you have experienced from the first day to the last. It will be interesting for you to see the ways in which your perceptions may or may not have changed. Next, try to sort your notes according to a set of topics or categories. The topics may come forth as you study your data or you may have set up a predetermined list of observation categories. Then, use a color-coding system to mark or highlight similar data. As you are working, it is possible that you will discover that you need to add new categories or revise existing ones.

We suggested that when you begin your observations, you should separate your field notes from your interpretations, judgments, and questions. The next task is to review these notes and align them with the data you have organized into categories. It is at this point that you can determine whether or not you can support your assessments. Does the data match your conclusions? As you proceed to your analysis, draw on the wide range of viewpoints and theories you have met in your readings. Use your organized data to document, examine, and critique what you observed and read about, and try to reflect upon the multiple facets of teaching and learning that you have been exploring.

Although these steps may seem tedious and, yes, time consuming, they will help you create an authentic and accurate depiction of what you saw. The primary purpose of the portrait assignment is to offer you a format for synthesizing your observation experience. By examining and reflecting on what the experience has meant to you, we hope you will discover new implications for teaching and learning in various contexts. In developing these skills you will have expanded your abilities to be a researcher in your own classroom, constantly attentive to your students' needs and progress. To extend the ramifications of your observation consider the following questions:

> *What elements do you believe form an ideal teaching-learning environment? What goals would you consider to be most important? What resources should be included? What would the setting look like?*

CHAPTER 7

Who Needs Grades Anyway?
Assessment, Evaluation, and Grading

In the very first sentence of the first chapter of this text, we used the word *controversies* to characterize the educational milieu at the start of the 21st century. In subsequent chapters, we cited a catalog of controversies surrounding the learning process, the issues of diversity, and the differing expectations for teachers and students. One might have thought that these were more than enough controversies for prospective educators to deal with.

Unfortunately, there is yet another topic with serious consequences fueling the educational debates. To complicate matters, there is even controversy around the terminology used in these debates. The multiplicity of terms employed, some undefined and others used interchangeably, tends to interfere with both communication and decision making. Before you proceed with this chapter, jot down your answers to the following questions:

How should learning be measured? How do you distinguish between assessment and evaluation? What purposes do tests serve? What is authentic assessment? What are rubrics and what purposes do they serve? What do grades communicate? What is accountability and to whom should students and teachers be held accountable?

In this chapter, we examine the terminology, the various ways in which learning is identified, and several of the underlying assumptions embedded in specific terms. We illustrate how assessment and evaluation are integrated and implemented in our philosophy.

Assessment versus Evaluation

Although it is quite common to find the terms *assessment* and *evaluation* used synonymously, we believe that there are advantages to clearly distinguishing between them. We assert that assessment incorporates a continuum of approaches designed to identify students as learners. Assessment studies students' achievements, academic strengths and needs, intelligences, learning styles, and socioemotional development. Assessment is a continuous process that informs learners, teachers, and parents about students' progress and proposed next steps.

We agree with the work of Andrew Stibbs (1979) and his vision that assessment entails different methods of assessment for different purposes. These include diagnosing, monitoring, screening, planning, describing, predicting, grading, and reporting. He proposes that assessment be viewed on two spectra, from public to private uses, and from measuring to describing methods. "Sometimes, for instance, descriptive assessments such as profiles, may be of more use to the public, and the observations on which they are based of more use to the teacher, than are standardized test results" (p. 69).

Within our umbrella definition of assessment, and consistent with Stibbs's analysis, the term *evaluation* is a form of judgment, a set of conclusions. Sometimes the conclusions are made by the teacher-as-examiner in the form of a grade, but in today's high-stakes testing era, standardized test scores can determine and override the teacher's informed appraisal.

In a climate that emphasizes student and teacher accountability, and with a growing emphasis on performance standards, we are all challenged to rethink the definitions, roles, and purposes of assessment and evaluation. Somehow, without losing our philosophical bearings, we need to find ways to align the existing standards and assessment policies with our practice.

The Pros and Cons of Standardized Testing

The first thing we want do is distinguish among *standards, standardized testing,* and *standardization.*

Standards

If we consider such terms as expectations, goals, objectives, and benchmarks for learning as synonyms for standards, then we have always had standards. Unfortunately, they have come to represent an inflexible, agreed-upon, and acceptable level of achievement or attainment for all students regardless of differences. Over time, they may have changed to reflect societal needs and emerging new knowledge, but the point is that education has never been "standardless." Nor should it be. The problem is that a standards movement has emerged that tends to constrict and constrain teaching and learning in arbitrary and narrowing ways. Mayher (1999) writes:

It would be interesting to see what such standards might look like if the focus was on students as future citizens and happy human beings, including but not limited to their needs for future education and their contribution to economic prosperity. The narrowness of the traditional conception of standards we've all assumed from the disciplinary bases has robbed us of a chance to think more broadly about the people we'd like our children to be. (p. 117)

The value of standards has been undermined by the emergence of too many sets of standards produced by too many commissions, states, and professional associations, inundating teachers and curriculum developers with long lists, not always compatible with one another. The final blow to a perfectly fine idea is that standards are now linked to a vast array of standardized tests intended only to measure ends at the expense of means.

Standardized Tests

Although there are several types of standardized tests, we are concerned here with standardized achievement tests, the paper-and-pencil type of instruments designed to determine students' knowledge of a particular body of content at a particular age or grade level. These tests are developed by commercial testing companies or educational agencies that have applied statistical tools to meet reliability and validity criteria. Though standardized test-makers claim that their products are keyed to the standards, often this is not the case because the standards and the curricula differ from school to school and state to state. W. James Popham (2001) presents three arguments against using standardized tests to evaluate the quality of students' schooling:

There are meaningful mismatches between what is tested and what is supposed to be taught, and those mismatches are often unrecognized. (p. 46)

The quest for wide score-spread tends to eliminate items covering important content that teachers have emphasized and students have mastered. (p. 48)

Factors other than instruction also influence students' performance on these tests. (p. 74)

Nevertheless, scores have serious consequences not only for the students themselves but also for their teachers and schools. While it is generally agreed that no single evaluation measure should be the basis for decision making, standardized tests are appropriately described as "high stakes" because they are being used as the single determinant of students' promotion and graduation, teachers' evaluations, and federal and state funding. And, because the stakes are high, the tests have come to drive the curriculum rather than the curriculum driving the tests. The time-consuming task of test preparation prepares students to become good test-takers. The art of teaching that turns them into avid lifelong learners and questioners of the world around them is more and more absent.

Linda McNeil's research (2000) and Alfie Kohn's indictment of standardized testing (1999, 2000) show that these tests measure what matters least, do not reveal information about levels of thinking, cannot assess teaching or learning, and have harmful effects on diverse groups of students. Standardized tests contribute to the dropout rate, to teacher disillusionment, and to damaging comparisons between schools and school districts. Last, but not least, they foster standardization, a one-size-fits-all conception of the goals of education.

Standardized tests also have become widespread in teacher certification systems. Although state regulatory agencies have imposed stringent standards on the colleges and universities that offer teacher education programs, students who are about to graduate from these institutions must also achieve satisfactory results on state-mandated examinations in order to obtain their teaching certificates. Some states use the National Teacher Examination whereas other states have created their own tests. And, in a few states, periodic testing of inservice teachers is also required.

Standardization

Arbitrary standards and standardized tests have resulted in a context of standardization that neither accounts for nor respects individual differences among learners. From our perspective, standardization implies uniformity, sameness, and regularity. When applied to enacting an educational program, it confirms the assumption that all learners should receive the same curriculum and be held to the same expectations. The result is what Peter Sacks (1999) decries as "standardized minds." Diversity, as we explored it in Chapter 4, takes second place, frequently leading to Susan Ohanian's claim that *one size fits few* (1999) and to Larry Cuban's (cited in Willis, 2002) conclusion: "Today, the idea of customizing runs hard against the strong impulse for uniformity and standardization in schooling that has grown in this country during the past 20 years" (p. 6). Such assembly-line education ignores the extraordinary talents and diverse thinkers among children who may become tomorrow's artists, scientists, financiers, and politicians.

As we also noted, one of the distinguishing features of schooling in the United States has always been its designation as a state responsibility. Each of the 50 states has its own structure, legislative mandates, requirements for certifying teachers, and procedures for monitoring schools and schooling. Admittedly this can be an unwieldy arrangement, especially as we become an increasingly mobile society. But state jurisdiction has also been the way to ensure that each state provided education appropriate for its particular population of students. However, it will take continuous pressure from parents and educators to guarantee that provisions will be appropriately maintained for all children and youth.

The extent to which variations in curriculum content and differentiated instructional approaches are recommended and implemented depends largely upon the importance placed on respecting diversity in all its dimensions. Standardization is a distorted belief in equality and enforces a system to which all children, regardless of their differences, are held accountable.

What do you believe standardized test scores communicate? What role did standardized tests play in your schooling? To what extent do you think standardized tests revealed your abilities, knowledge, and skills?

For an in-depth and powerful critique of the widespread, mandated use of standardized testing in the state of Texas, we recommend Linda M. McNeil's study (2000), *Contradictions of School Reform: Educational Costs of Standardized Testing.* In her own words, and with her own italics, she sends us a frightening message:

> The sound bytes that seduce policymakers always emphasize claims of benefits, not the actual costs. As documented in this book, the costs are great: a decline in the quality of what is taught and a new form of discrimination in the education of poor and minority kids. But perhaps the worst effect is the silencing of two voices most important in understanding the real effects of standardization: the teachers and the children. (p. xxi)

In her concluding chapter, McNeil alerts us to the dangers that lurk when standardized testing takes control:

> It is critical to note that the effects of the Texas Accountability System, in de-skilling teachers, restratifying access to education, and, in incipient ways, de-democratizing education, are not flaws in the system. They are the logical consequences of the system when it is working. It is the purpose of the accountability system to render education into a technical enterprise, one that is less owned by the public and less hampered by the inefficiencies of democratic debate. And one of its intended purposes may be to limit the education of the least powerful among our young people. (p. 270)

Though many educators work to counteract the reliance on student evaluation through standardized testing, at the federal level there appears to be increased attention to support this practice. Educators opposing standardized testing see this as undermining and eradicating successful school reform initiatives such as alternative schools, charter schools, and the small schools movement. Furthermore, such tests arbitrarily sort students, strongly influence the content of the curricula, and force teachers to devote large segments of class time to test preparation.

Classroom Assessment

Our concern about standardized testing does not mean that we reject all kinds of testing, assessments, and evaluations. On the contrary, teachers and parents need to know how and what their learners are learning. Teachers can use a variety of approaches to accomplish this, while simultaneously learning how successful their teaching has been and the extent to which they have enabled their students to become partners in learning.

Teachers can gain information through observations, discussions, oral and written reports, and students' journals. They can devise short quizzes and essay tests, hold individual conferences, and maintain inventories. By examining files of students' work they will be able to trace their students' development over time. The main point is that multiple measures situated in the classroom context, related to the curriculum under study, and including thoughtful student work, will lead to an holistic picture of students' accomplishments, strengths, and needs.

Multiple assessments also give teachers clues about how they are teaching and how their students are learning. If students' written and oral responses show confusion or a lack of understanding, teachers should be prompted to question their own actions, methods and approaches. Their discoveries should challenge them to rethink their planning and help them assess their own progress toward meeting their various instructional goals. At the same time, they will gain rich data for communicating with their learners, their learners' parents, and the public at large.

Authentic Assessment

For teachers and students, authentic assessment is among the least recognized and valued. It is far more demanding than standardized testing because it requires that students and teachers regularly question and communicate how and what is being learned, the extent to which learners are improving, growing, and expanding what they know, and the directions that will lead to their further growth and knowledge. Authentic assessment is an individualized, interactive process whereby students demonstrate their understandings, and teachers offer guidance toward further progress. Both teachers and students are most often rewarded by their participation in such a process. Unfortunately, nowhere in any set of standards is there any mention of students taking personal responsibility for their learning or taking pleasure in the teaching and learning process.

Grant Wiggins (1990), a strong advocate of authentic assessment, makes the case concisely:

. . . the move to reform assessment is based upon the premise that assessment should primarily support the needs of learners. Thus, secretive tests composed of proxy items and scores that have no obvious meaning or usefulness undermine teachers' ability to improve instruction and students' ability to improve their performance. (p. 2)

In their article "Authentic Assessment: Beyond the Buzzword and into the Classroom" (1991), Rieneke Zessoules and Howard Gardner emphasize that authentic assessment must be seen as a culture:

In summary, authentic assessment involves a complicated reevaluation of classroom activities and responsibilities . . . changing the kinds of activities students engage in . . . altering the responsibilities of students and teachers in increasingly sophisticated ways, and transforming the static, mechanical, and disengaging moments when learning stops and testing begins into a continuum of moments that combine assessment, instruction, and learning. . . . No longer a weapon for rooting out and combating students' weaknesses, assessment becomes an additional occasion for learning—a tool for students, as much as for teachers, parents, and administrators to discover strengths, possibilities, and future directions in students' work. (p. 63)

What opportunities have you had, in and out of school, to engage in authentic assessment? How might authentic assessment help learners deepen their awareness of their own achievements and guide them in their studies? What are the differences between preparing for a standardized test and engaging in authentic assessment?

Developing, Negotiating, and Applying Assessment Criteria

Authentic assessment, as contrasted with standardized testing and its claims of objectivity, is often criticized for being "soft and fuzzy," relying too much on goodwill and too little on evidence that stated expectations have been satisfied. Moreover, generalized statements of assessment—excellent, good, poor—either communicate nothing to students and their parents or are open to wide interpretation. These flaws occur because the criteria for assessment have not been developed, made explicit, or applied with consistency.

When criteria are negotiated between teachers and their students the criteria are likely to be reasonably and clearly understood. The process of negotiation gives students greater control over their learning, a better sense of the goals of their course, clear directions for how they can meet these goals, and a sense of personal responsibility. There are no secrets or surprises. All learners can participate in articulating the expectations and describing the behaviors that determine their progress as learners.

Rubrics

A rubric is an authentic assessment tool that can be used to guide, measure, and document students' progress. Using rubrics can create an ongoing process by inviting students to participate in the rubric's design, guiding them in their self-assessment, and fostering collaboration between them and their teachers. For example, the process of creating a rubric for a project helps students to see what they need to do to best fulfill the assignment. Rubrics focus the teacher on clarifying criteria in specific terms, and in showing students what is expected of them and how their work will be evaluated. Most attractive to students is that rubrics provide a schema to rate performance by indicating the degree to which an assignment, project, or standard has been met.

According to Wiggins (1998), a rubric is a set of scoring guidelines for evaluating students' work. Rubrics answer the following questions:

By what criteria should performance be judged?

Where should we look and what should we look for to judge performance success?

What does the range in the quality of performance look like?

How do we determine validly, reliably, and fairly what score should be given and what that score means?

How should the different levels of quality be described and distinguished from one another? (p. 154)

Rubrics can be overused. A different rubric for each assignment in each class poses the danger that learning will be fragmented and creativity will be squelched. The specificity of rubrics can deny the opportunity for trial and error or inhibit risk taking. Opportunities for "the having of wonderful ideas" will be lost. Rubrics are not a panacea for all aspects of assessment and accountability; they should be used with discretion.

On another scale, a rubric can be seen as a single, overarching tool to be employed throughout a course or semester. We think of it as a contract between teachers and students, one that will work only if all parties have a hand in shaping it and everybody understands the mutual obligation it imposes. In that sense, the rubric implicitly measures the performance of teachers too, inasmuch as they promise to set things up and maintain them in a certain way. As a class proceeds, it should revisit the rubric from time to time, sometimes making changes or refining it.

Looking at One's Self

Self-assessment is a key component of authentic assessment. It represents a commitment to students' participation in assessing their progress and their learning. Ways to engage students in self-assessment include weekly reflections, self-reports, double-entry journals, and peer and teacher conferences.

Reflection

Written reflections can play a major role for both teachers and students. These reflections give students the opportunity to explore the uniqueness of their ideas. Student comments help teachers see how students interpret classroom experiences. This information guides teachers in future planning and helps them see the divergent ways in which students express their learning and draw their conclusions. Additionally, this process presents the possibility of creating more democratic classrooms. Teachers can benefit from the pool of ideas their students offer and reconsider the paths that need to be taken.

Self-Assessment

Written and oral self-assessments are substantive opportunities for students to examine critically, revise, and communicate what and how they are learning. For example, a midpoint self-assessment is the chance to say "This is where I am right now. This is what I am thinking about. The following readings have helped me formulate some ideas. These are the goals I want to pursue during the remainder of the semester." Similarly, a final self-assessment invites students to show their growth and development from the first to the last day of the class. To the same end, younger children and students with diverse learning styles may more easily communicate their progress in one-on-one dialogues with their teacher.

The real import of self-assessments comes as students probe, analyze, and synthesize the meanings they are making by exploring how resources, class discussions, activities, and assignments may have influenced their growth or understandings. For this to occur, students must be encouraged to convey the depth of their involvement, the insights they have derived, and the issues or ideas that have been raised for them. It may seem that these methods and analyses are geared to adolescents and adults, but they are not. Young children are equally articulate, knowledgeable, imaginative, and aware of themselves as learners; given the opportunity and encouragement they are all too willing to share what they know. Students should not hesitate to describe their accomplishments but should be reminded that self-assessments are not intended as occasions for self-glorification At the same time, they should try to acknowledge their limitations and identify ways in which they might improve.

Note too that self-assessments provide students with a concrete basis for discussion with peers, teachers, and parents. They can be used to develop plans, solve problems, or refocus energies. Because each student's starting point may be different, we suggest examining progress as occurring on a continuum. This respects the uniqueness of each individual's growth.

Portfolios

Although school authorities and college admissions officers continue to deliberate about how to weigh student portfolios in determining academic achievements or in making decisions about entrance to an institution of higher education, there is a high degree of agreement among teachers, school administrators, and teacher educators that portfolios are effective in assessing students' growth and learning.

The portfolio is a means for students to define themselves as learners, and to convey their understandings through documentation of their work. Just as artists' portfolios are representations of their accomplishments, students' portfolios reveal their accomplishments and achievements. Most important, the portfolio documents what and how an individual learned over time. David Perkins (1992) offers a concise description:

> A portfolio is a selective enterprise. Not everything goes into it, just those items that students think most powerfully reflect their understandings and their expressions of those understandings. The portfolio functions as an object of review and assessment for the teacher, but also as a gauge of progress and occasion of reflection for the learner. (p. 137)

Teachers can help students in the preparation of their portfolios by assisting them in the selection of the items to be included and in organizing, illustrating, and formatting their documents. Most important, students should be advised about analyzing and reflecting on the items they submit. Learning portfolios may vary across schools, classrooms, and grade levels but in all cases they should contain representative work and artifacts that define each individual learner.

As Campbell et al. (2001) write about the prospective teacher's portfolio: "To be powerful, a portfolio must be a truthful self-portrait that gives others an accurate picture of where you are in the lifelong journey of professional development" (p. 49).

Whaddya Get? From Assessment to Evaluation and Grading

Despite the lapse in time and the phonetic differences between the spelling of the subheading above and the title of the book, *WAD-J-GET? The Grading Game in American Education,* by Howard Kirschenbaum, Sidney B. Simon, and Rodney W. Napier (1971), the concern is the same. "Grading is one of the most controversial topics in American education" (p. 14). In a fictionalized examination of the issues as they unfolded in the 1960s, these authors show students, teachers, parents, administrators, and alumni voicing a range of viewpoints and grappling with the dilemmas grading poses. Can creativity be graded? Does effort count? Do grades force students to learn things that don't interest them? Do grades lead to emphasizing the content that is easily measurable? Do grades pit students against each other? Does grading get in the way of learning? Does grading stifle creativity and divergent thinking?

Grading, whether or not you agree with it, plays a weighty role in students' lives. With the competition for acceptance at colleges and universities, we add other questions: how do admissions officers make sense of grades? To what extent does their suspicion of grade inflation lead them to greater dependency on standardized test scores?

It may be true that grades are a manageable shorthand and that they fit easily on report cards and college transcripts. Yet, both letter and numerical grades are highly symbolic indicators open to multiple interpretations. Even when letters and numbers are linked with such terms as *excellent, good, satisfactory,* and so forth, we still have to wonder what meanings are actually being conveyed. Do these indicators mean the same to one teacher as to another? Do parents and students understand the differences between what different teachers are communicating?

Joseph P. McDonald (1996) argues that grading "stifles opportunities for deeper teaching and learning" and that "there is little scientific basis for assuming reliability" (p. 114).

In fact, there is rarely anything more than private and subjective judgment underlying all the analysis: whether to deduct five points or no points for failure to indent paragraphs or label angles, whether to put weight on the book reports or on class partici-pation, whether book reports are even a very good way to assess reading, whether to count effort. The reliability of such a grading procedure across students, teachers, grades and courses—that is, the likelihood that one A or C is equal to another—is ut-ter illusion because different graders are typically not linked by even the barest con-versation about standards. (p. 114)

The use of grading has insidious consequences even beyond the disparities among the in-dividuals to whom they are applied and by whom they are interpreted. As professors, we would ask our preservice students to describe themselves as elementary or secondary school learners. When they responded with statements such as "I was a C student" or "My GPA was 3.5," we realized that they had internalized the labels; the labels had come to be who they were. They were just as endangered as George Bernard Shaw's flower girl, unable to see them-selves for who they really are and who they can become.

Earlier we described a rubric as a set of criteria. In our teaching experiences, we learned that after students and teachers have lived through several months of applying and revising these criteria, they find it is possible to use the rubric to define a specific grade in terms of the agreed-upon criteria. The rubric became a collaboratively constructed tool that guided student performance and assessment. We worked at constructing such rubrics and developed assign-ments that provided students with multiple opportunities to demonstrate their growing knowl-edge. Students, in turn, discussed ways in which they could design rubrics in their various field placements.

While admitting our reservations, we have come to accept the reality that grades are firmly institutionalized. Even as we aim to reduce the dependency on grades, we seek to ensure ways to make them meaningful through multiple forms of feedback including individual confer-ences with opportunities for students and teachers to discuss how grades were determined. We maintain that only when grading is coupled with qualitative feedback does the learner have a full assessment of his or her work.

Overall, we believe that the process of grading will always be controversial. The stress of high stakes testing looms over students and teachers across the country. Simultaneously, many teachers are struggling to find the time and the space in their curricula to engage and energize their students in motivating, meaningful, and challenging dimensions of learning, believing these efforts will foster the students' personal growth and reflect genuine authentic assessment.

In your experience as a student, what grades were most meaningful? Why? If rubrics appeared in your classroom, how were they used and who was responsible for creating them? As a future teacher, which aspects of grading are most important to you?

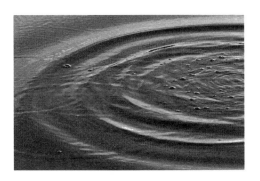

CHAPTER 8

Schools, Schooling, and School Reform

American education is neither monolithic nor fixed, but always in a state of change. Any attempt to understand the contemporary scene requires that we take at least a brief look at what preceded, a daunting task because, as Adolpe E. Meyer (1965) explains, "educational history at bottom is social history."

> . . . it is also the history of philosophy and psychology, of teaching methods of school organization, of school support and maintenance, of politics and law. Nor should it be forgotten that it concerns itself not only with social forces, but also with people, especially those involved in one way or another in numerous transactions, whether as consumers or dispensers, whether commoners or peers, and especially, of course, with its immortal great, its singular men and women, its spinners of dreams—even seers. (p. 1)

It is almost impossible and probably not desirable to isolate the concept of "school" from its interlocking social, political, and economic surroundings. Without going into great detail, this chapter presents a picture of the contexts in which schools developed and how they evolved.

The Ongoing Transformation of American Schools

The schools of the United States are as diverse as the population attending them. Each of the 50 states, and in many cases each municipality within each state, has its own regulations, tax structure, monitoring and accountability systems, and requirements for students and for teachers. To this mix also must be added the many variations among the independent schools and the schools supported by religious denominations.

Although these differences may seem confusing and incoherent, there is a legal common denominator. Federal law has clearly established the right of every child to a free public education and the responsibility of each state to provide support for that education. In 1954, the Supreme Court's decision in the case of *Brown v. Board of Education of Topeka, Kansas* laid the ground-work for equal educational opportunities for all students by mandating school desegregation.

The country's continuing changing demographics led to the 1968 Bilingual Education Act, which mandated that bilingual education receive federal funding through Title VII of the Elementary and Secondary Education Act. When Title VII expired in 2002, it was transformed into Title III, becoming the English Language Acquisition Language Enhancement and Academic Achievement Act. Whereas Title VII allowed children to learn in their native language, Title III focuses specifically on English language learning and fosters English only.

Title IX of the Education Amendments of 1972 to the Civil Rights Act of 1964 marked prohibition against gender discrimination. The implementation of Title IX has dramatically affected athletic programs and scholarships and protects students and teachers from sexual harassment.

It was not until 1975, however, that Public Law 94–142 provided federally guaranteed rights for all handicapped children in public schools. Its main thrust was to integrate special-needs students with their general education peers in a "least restrictive environment" setting.

Clearly, the variations in how these laws have been implemented reflect both the state and federal government's commitments and their capacity to serve the wide-ranging needs of its citizens at different times under different local and worldwide conditions.

We acknowledge, as did Lawrence A. Cremin (1966), that "the genius of American education—its animating spirit, its most distinctive quality—lies in the commitment to popularization" (Preface). At the same time, we have to concede that American education, as Henry J. Perkinson (1968) claimed, is an "imperfect panacea," because " faith in the power of education has led all of us to make unwarranted, unrealistic, and harmful demands upon it" (Preface). Indeed, there have been accomplishments, but they do not absolve us from facing up to the weaknesses, the problems, and the obstacles that have prevented us from fully meeting our goals. No school is impervious to some or all of the following social conditions: changing social values, demographic shifts, the technological revolution, inequalities in the distribution of resources, disaffection among many young people, the worldwide impact of terrorism, a rising pattern of violence, high levels of unemployment, poverty, the HIV/AIDS epidemic, and numerous other widespread diseases and serious illnesses. The "social inequalities" that Jonathan Kozol (1991) reveals, the "contradictions of control" that Linda McNeil (1986) uncovers, and the "compromises" Theodore Sizer's English teacher must make (1984) are but three of the multiple difficulties that educators confront within an increasingly demanding world of schooling.

This chapter explores turning points in the history of American schooling, highlights some of the major issues plaguing our schools, examines some of the dilemmas parents, students, and teachers face, and reports on a few of the possibilities with potential to strengthen our schools.

How would you describe the schools you attended? Did anyone ever explain to you why the schools you attended were structured as they were? In what ways were your schools responsive to your needs? What kinds of changes were taking place in your community and in what ways did they affect your schooling?

Looking Back

Educational historians, from Ellwood P. Cubberly (1919) to Lawrence A. Cremin (1988) to James W. Fraser (2001), have traced and documented events and stages of growth in the evolution of American education. They cite among the early contributing factors European influences, religious motives, guiding democratic principals, the formal establishment of governing bodies, expanding national boundaries, population growth, and economic trends. They point out that starting from the middle of the 19th century, schooling showed the effects of immigration, secularization, industrialization, suffrage, urbanization, and the dissemination of research in the growing field of psychology, and often reflected a struggle for power between elite and popular movements. They note, too, that corresponding changes occurred in the types of schools created, in the curricula content chosen, and in the instructional processes introduced. What and how teaching and learning should be enacted was, and continues to be, influenced by learning theories, by the distribution of new knowledge, by the accessibility and impact of the media, and by emerging global political, economic, and social pressures.

Rather than attempt to encapsulate in a few pages all that occurred since the pre-Revolutionary period, we have selected events that have endured. In the span of a little more than 200 years, schooling in America has been transformed. The one-room schoolhouses of frontier days and the religious control of the early settlers have given way to numerous public and private educational settings and institutions to accommodate learning from infancy through adulthood.

Gradually states enacted laws mandating compulsory schooling and levied taxes to support it, though there were, and still are, too many unmet needs. In addition to the Supreme Court decision in *Brown v. the Board of Education* and the enactment and subsequent reauthorizations of the laws we previously cited, American education in the 20th century changed significantly in a myriad of directions.

Alfred Binet's publishing of the first mental measurement scales on intelligence in 1905 led to a still to this day frenzy of activity regarding the development and employment of tests to measure intelligence, skills, knowledge, aptitudes, and attitudes. The No Child Left Behind Act of 2001 may be the penultimate result of the apparent need to measure what students are learning and to hold teachers accountable.

The establishment of the first junior high school in 1909 generated a movement that has led to the emergence of middle schools and junior high schools in districts across the country.

Ironically, after 100 years of development, some educators are questioning the value of these schools and advocating a return to the eight year elementary school and four year high school. It seems fair to ask to what extent these proposals are prompted by serious considerations of the nature of the early adolescent or by emphases on the transmission of subject matter content to satisfy the persistent pressure of testing.

Another frenzy of activity was sparked in 1957 by the launching of the Sputnik satellite, setting off a series of educational reforms focusing on the structure of the disciplines, most specifically in mathematics and the sciences. Until this event, support for education had been the sole responsibility of the states, but anxiety concerning America's ability to compete with the Soviet Union led, in 1958, to the first major intrusion by the federal government, the passage of the National Defense Education Act, resulting in federal funding for public education.

1965 marked both the passing of the Elementary and Secondary Education Act (ESEA), bringing programs to public schools, and the creation of Project Head Start, a program to provide comprehensive services to low-income preschoolers so that they would be ready to succeed when they entered elementary school (Zigler & Styfco, 1993).

In turn, Head Start stimulated the growth of day care centers, preschools and nursery schools nationwide. Infant schools, transplanted from England and initiated by early settlers during the 17th century, soon were translated into American primary schools. Kindergartens, as the entry level for most elementary school children, began to appear during the late 19th century, but gradually were introduced into public schools in more affluent communities and then eventually into most school systems.

Senior high schools, first conceived as schools for college-bound students, became comprehensive schools with curricula designed for those planning to enter the workforce as well as for those headed for higher education or the ministry. From its inception, high school became a sorting mechanism, distinguishing students from different social classes into workers and scholars. Yet, when James Bryant Conant, a former president of Harvard University, conducted a series of investigations (1959, 1967), he reported that many schools did not offer the wide array of courses required to meet the needs of all students. He recommended that comprehensive high schools offer more courses for the academically talented, encourage girls to study mathematics and the sciences, and provide more vocational education for the "nonacademic" students. The large, all-inclusive high school became the model for student success. As we note later in this chapter, Conant's solutions are now challenged by proponents of small schools, magnet schools, alternative schools, and schools for special populations.

Goals and Purposes

Over the course of our educational history the purposes of schooling came to be identified with leading statesmen, strong political figures, influential educators, and burgeoning professional associations. Each individual or organization mirrored the circumstances of a particular era, but as a group they represented a political and intellectual spectrum, bequeathing to us the proverbial swinging pendulum of change and reform. Were we to choose a single individual whose influence has endured, we would argue that despite the views of some educational critics, John Dewey's contributions have made the most lasting impression. His visions permeate models of teaching and learning in the present and for the future. Dewey (1900) wrote:

> The obvious fact is that our social life has undergone a thorough and radical change. If our education is to have any meaning for life, it must pass through an equally complete transformation. To do this means to make each one of our schools an embryonic community life, active with types of occupations that reflect the life of the larger society and permeated throughout with the spirit of art, history, and science. When the school introduces and trains each child of society into membership within such a little community, saturating him with the spirit of service, and providing him with the instruments of effective self-direction we shall have the deepest and best guaranty of a larger society which is worthy, lovely, and harmonious. (pp. 28–29)

With the passage of time, multiple curricula and teaching models have come and gone with the swinging pendulum, but teacher preparation programs across the country continue to devote attention to the enactment of Dewey's philosophy of looking at the world through honest questioning, real-life study, and experimentation.

As the country grew and circumstances changed, educators, philosophers, and politicians continued to battle and to propose new curricula. Schools took on the burden of meeting expanding and often conflicting objectives. They assumed responsibility for preparing a technically skilled, academically educated, culturally enriched, and emotionally and physically healthy citizenry. Illustrative of the expanding and often incompatible statements of goals are the numerous reports that appeared in the single year of 1983. The Education Commission of the States (1983) summarized 10 reports on how to improve education, and Griesemer and Butler (1983), under the auspices of the Northeast Regional Exchange, analyzed 8 of the 10 reports. What becomes most apparent is that the goals and purposes of education are riddled with conflicting tensions and belief systems. Tyack and Cuban (1995) describe Americans as wanting "schools to serve different and often contradictory purposes for their own children:"

> To socialize them to be obedient, yet to teach them to be critical thinkers.
>
> To pass on the best academic knowledge that the past has to offer, yet also to teach marketable and practical skills.
>
> To cultivate cooperation, yet to teach students to compete with one another in school and later in life.
>
> To stress basic skills but also encourage creativity and higher-order thinking.
>
> To focus on the academic "basics," yet to permit a wide range of choice of courses. (p. 43)

Because most Americans have come to believe that education provides the means to solve society's problems and to ensure each individual's future success, they have placed substantial faith in its ability to cure all ills. Sadly, it is not so simple. Public schools from coast to coast vary in their vantage points regarding what will best address their problems, but the political climate determines whose goals will be met. Academic goals are only a fraction of what schools must incorporate into their daily agendas; yet, in most schools the academic emphases loom over the heads of students and teachers alike.

The No Child Left Behind Act of 2001

As a case in point, we call attention to the parameters and hurdles surrounding the federal education legislation, the No Child Left Behind Act of 2001(NCLB). The thrust of this Act requires that schools and teachers be held accountable for student achievement. All teachers must be highly qualified in their subject areas and states are required to submit a plan to ensure this. States must develop and administer annual testing in reading and math from grades 3–8, identify and define student proficiency levels, and furnish annual report cards showing student achievement data. In 2006 such testing will be extended through the 11th grade of high school. States must also compete for grants to receive monies for *Reading First,* a program designed for children in grades K–3. States can also apply for funds to create reading programs for children ages 3–5. The law further stipulates that all reading programs must meet the criterion of being based on scientific research. NCLB monies are prescribed for Title I, for the improvement of teacher quality, and for bilingual education. One might be surprised to learn that a law claiming to leave no child behind leaves many behind.

The institutionalization of high-stakes testing has created havoc. A school's success is now measured by the ubiquitous, single test, a measure that does not take into account the differences among children. All children are looked at arbitrarily, be they gifted, handicapped, rich, or poor. The tragedy is that the children who have the farthest to go to succeed are those who fare the least well in a test score race. Their lives and the lives of their teachers become a daily routine of teaching to the test. The vast domain of a full and complete education is abandoned for the pencil-test performance.

Many teachers, administrators, students, and parents are highly frustrated by the impact of this law. Ironically, many of the highly qualified teachers the law seeks to retain are leaving the profession as they see their reasons for teaching falling by the wayside. Parents are discovering that in order to add more class time for test preparation, subjects such as music, art, and even recess have been scrapped from the school day. Play and its many academic and social components are no longer valued in the classroom. Newer, more authentic systems of evaluation such as portfolios are becoming fatalities.

Whereas major funding is supposed to assist communities that most need it, it is these diverse groups who are most discouraged. Test scores cannot be raised higher or fast enough for students and schools to be called successful. In some cases, states have withdrawn their applications for funding to alleviate these pressures. The re-election of President George W. Bush in November 2004 has sustained and extended his NCLB Act.

Controversial Initiatives

The agenda so clearly prescribed by NCLB has also reinforced several other educational initiatives, including vouchers, privatization, home schooling, and school choice.

Vouchers. Vouchers enable parents to draw on education dollars and spend them at private schools, appear to be a means by which parents can participate in school choice. Parents in struggling school districts see vouchers as an opportunity to put their children in more successful schools than the ones in which their children are currently enrolled. In some cases, their search for safer environments leads to their choosing religious schools or private schools. Critics claim that vouchers weaken the public school system and defy democratic practices. Furthermore, vouchers are somewhat misleading in that they often do not cover full tuition costs. Makani Themba-Nixon (2003) contends that vouchers are "the ultimate breach in the social contract," as well as an effort to counter school integration.

Privatization. Also known as contracting, privatization is a system by which schools are operated, controlled, and managed by for-profit firms or independent organizations under contract with public authorities. Although privatization is not a new idea in the public sector, it is somewhat new to education. Contracts vary regarding an array of criteria. Some contracts indicate that the company must ensure that students will meet the established state standards. Agreements usually give the company control of the curriculum content and methods of instruction and are authorized to select teachers free of any union obligations. Contracts almost always include the company's commitment to supply instructional resources, teaching materials, books, and computers. The unique complexities of schools has often stymied the success of this model. In some instances for-profit firms have failed because they did not adequately understand school culture. Teachers, a leading force in the day-to-day activity of schools, see their roles as educators cut or diminished and teacher unions suffer an enormous loss of power. Opponents perceive this system as simply another way for "profit-seeking companies to get their hands on a bigger share of the . . . billion-a-year K–12 education 'industry' " (Miner, 2003, p. 176). On the other hand, there have been reports of only limited financial gains for most of these companies. Contrary to expectations, only modest profits have been accrued by a few of the companies and the Edison Schools, the biggest for-profit firm, lost more than 233.5 million in the preceding decade (Miner, p. 177).

Home Schooling. We all know that parents are a child's first teachers. Yet, of all the modern variations on schooling, home schooling may be the least well known and the most controversial. Although the courts have never officially ruled on the issue of home schooling, it has been widely recognized over the past 20 years and is presently a growing movement with legal status, though regulations vary from state to state (Lines, 1995; Reich, 2002). The most distinguishing features of home schooling are that it is home-based and parent-led. It accommodates the wide range of special-needs children, involves high- and low-income families, parents with advanced and limited education, people of different ethnic, religious, and cultural backgrounds, and those geographically distanced from schools. Parents tend to choose to home school their children for social, academic, family, and/or religious reasons (Jeub, 1994). Supporters of home schooling claim that the home presents a natural environment in which parents are able to customize a child's education (Ray, 2002). Recent research shows that today the Christian right comprises the largest population of home schoolers, whereas home schooling in the 1970s reflected a liberal, democratic thrust. Home schooling has become an organized movement with communication networks and curriculum resources.

Critics of home schooling are concerned that children are not taught by professionals, are not exposed to the wealth of appropriate instructional materials, and do not participate in a formal system of assessment and evaluation. Socialization issues top this list. Experts worry that isolated children will not be able to adjust to a diverse society nor possess the ability to function in a workplace or team-based setting. Research shows, however, that home-schooled children are quite well adjusted and that many parents arrange social events and interactions with other children and even participate in selected school and community activities. Cooperative partnerships between parents and schools are rapidly growing.

School choice. School choice provides parents or guardians the opportunity to select their children's school. As in any form of choice, there are advantages and disadvantages and what seems a simple process is often surprisingly the opposite. School choice can mean anything from switching schools across town in a large city to using a voucher to enroll a child in a private or religious school, or selecting a high school with a specialized focus. One of the premises behind school choice is the hope that competition will be created and cause less popular, less effective schools to engage in serious self-improvement. However, the chances for strengthening the schools that are left behind are severely limited by the loss of motivated students who choose to leave. Furthermore, school choice is not easily enacted because navigating the bureaucracy is frustrating, desirable schools are overcrowded, and vouchers do not always fully satisfy the tuition requirements.

Sonia Nieto (2003), who sees many school initiatives as "hotly contested" at the national, state, and district levels, warns:

> Battles over vouchers, desegregation, privatization, and federal education policy reflect critical choices that will have a lasting impact not only on schools, but on public life as a whole and whether the United States will realize the promise of a pluralistic, multicultural democracy in the 21st century or abandon it. (p. vii)

Schools Reinventing Themselves

In one of the early studies of school change, Seymour Sarason (1971) noted " . . . any attempt to introduce change into the school setting requires, among other things, changing the existing regularities in some way . . . eliminating one or more of them, or producing new ones"

(p. 61). Educators, parents, and politicians have not been discouraged by the immensity of this task, and the drive to continue to shape and improve schools goes on. Like so much else in education, school reform has many faces. While reformers work to create unique new kinds of schools, the practices and attributes tend to cross over a variety of models. We try to highlight some of the individual characteristics of each, but you will surely see the ways in which they overlap.

Alternative Schools

Alternative schools is an umbrella term for many different types of nontraditional schools, public or private. Essentially these schools are designed as options for students who are not succeeding in conventional settings for a variety of different reasons, some of which may include disruptive and violent behavior, drugs, truancy, poor grades, school suspension, pregnancy, and a variety of mental health and emotional issues. Certain students choose alternative schools because they just do not fit the mold of the traditional setting. Some alternative schools are independent whereas others are attached to or are offshoots of a traditional school system. In some alternative settings, students work to return to the main school.

Alternative schools are usually smaller in size, working in tandem with a competent supportive staff of counselors, social workers, psychologists, and tutors. To address the needs of at-risk students, alternative schools try to attract dedicated and well-trained teachers, teachers who are flexible and willing to implement a variety of teaching strategies and effective curricula. These schools maintain a lower-than-average student-teacher ratio, enabling the teachers to work closely with their students. Alternative schools can also fit the categories of magnet schools, small schools, or charter schools.

Magnet Schools

Magnet schools, originally established to meet federal requirements for desegregation, are now serving the needs, interests, and abilities of many different student populations within the public sector. The underlying rationale is that all students do not learn in the same ways or in the same contexts and that when students want to be in a school of their choice they will do better in subjects unrelated to their particular bent.

In magnet schools, students are offered specialized curricula that evolve around a particular theme, or they are given opportunities for extensive study of selected content fields, or they may select to concentrate on the development of special talents. Intended to attract students of diverse backgrounds and designed to promote school integration, these schools aim to strengthen students' abilities while marketing their vocational skills or preparing them for higher education. In large cities, the number of magnet schools has grown considerably. As schools of choice they present positive options for students who want to devote their energies in particular directions while at the same time meeting general academic requirements.

Magnet schools exist at the elementary, middle, and high school levels. They may be restricted in size or quite large, and some schools require applicants to meet entrance criteria.

As is the case with other new school configurations, magnets also warrant criticism. Their success rates are challenged because they too cream off the best students from other schools and draw off resources needed by the nonmagnet schools. They are accused of elitism and are charged with tokenism because they use a selection process. Ironically, they are also seen as a new way to achieve segregation. But, in spite of the views of their detractors, magnet schools continue to gain in popularity.

Small Schools

Current arguments in favor of small schools are in sharp contrast to the concerns expressed by James Conant in the 1960s. Supported in part by the successful example of Deborah Meier (1995) at the Central Park East School, the small schools movement encompasses elementary, middle, junior high, and senior high schools. Common characteristics of small schools include heterogeneous student populations of 250 to 350 students; a cohesive self-selected faculty led by a teacher-director or principal; a high degree of autonomy around issues of curriculum, instruction, and assessment; a nonexclusive admissions policy; and strong parent participation. Sharply contrasting with the anonymity of larger, faceless schools, in small schools strong relationships develop among students, teachers, administrators, and members of the school community. Student attendance is higher and the intimate setting creates a nurturing and focused environment where students' needs and learning styles regularly can be met. Teachers, other school personnel, and parents collaborate on developing activities and instructional approaches, and by working together they get to know each other and their students. These experiences together with the opportunities to make decisions and decide policy create a strong sense of school ownership. In turn, ownership creates an even stronger sense of school commitment. Both the Carnegie and Gates Foundations have given considerable funding and support to nurture the small schools movement.

In summarizing the research on small schools, Michael Klonsky (1995) concluded that there was evidence that a small school:

Improves students' outcomes on grades and test scores.

Improves students' attendance rates and lowers drop-out rates.

Raises the success rate of female and nonwhite students.

Better serves special-need students, including the "at-risk," "exceptional," "disadvantaged," and "gifted."

Improves school security and lessens violence, alcohol and drug abuse. (p. 1).

Small schools have their downside as well. One problem faced by many small schools is finding a location. A number of small schools discover themselves housed together in what once was a large, single school building. Such situations are not without problems. The individual schools must figure out ways to share bathrooms, lunchrooms, gymnasiums, libraries, music and art rooms, and laboratories. Additionally, there may be inequity among the schools and one may have greater resources than the others. Those schools that cannot find space within a school find themselves renting space. In other cases, a large school decides to downsize and creates its own set of small schools within a school. Such change can be successful but also may cause disruption and competition.

A lack of resources and the ability to provide a wide range of course offerings present additional problems to small schools, and teachers are often responsible for teaching many grade levels in their subjects as well as electives. Despite all the problems, however, recent reports indicate that small schools are increasingly popular and are thriving with philanthropic donations and federal and state support (Hendrie, 2004).

Charter Schools

Of the several recent school restructurings that have surfaced, charter schools may be the most unique and prolific. They are defined as public schools, open to all who wish to attend, paid for with tax dollars, and held accountable for their results to an authoritative public body, as well as to those who enroll and teach in them (Manno, Finn, & Vanourek, p. 737). Their status as independent legal entities gives them the right to hire and fire, sue and be sued, award contracts for outside services, and control their finances (Bierlein, 1997, pp. 18–19).

Because anyone can create a charter school by following state guidelines, parents and teachers disillusioned by the bureaucratic nature of traditional schools have welcomed the chance to set their own educational priorities, develop a curriculum, select the staff free from teacher union interference, form the internal organization, and control the budget. Although starting and sustaining a charter school is fraught with stumbling blocks, these schools epitomize the concepts of freedom and choice that so many students, parents, teachers, and administrators seek.

Charter schools have prompted critical questions similar to those raised regarding other school innovations. The foes of charter schools employ a range of tactics to halt them. They add restrictions and red tape, insist upon adherence to regulations imposed on all other public schools, build alliances with teacher unions, claim neglect of children with disabilities, and demand evidence of improved learning outcomes. Additionally, they raise the claims of segregation and elitism, of promoting competition among schools, of having a negative impact on traditional schools, and of drawing off already limited state and local financial resources.

As a relatively new movement, charter schools are not yet on steady ground. Though they hold out great promise, many have already failed, possibly threatening the development of new ones (Schemo, 2004). With strong supporters and equally strong opponents, Good and Braden (2000) claim that only time will tell whether or not charter schools are another reform failure or a worthwhile investment.

Nonformal Educational Settings

Teaching and learning never has been limited to what happens inside school buildings, but now educators are recognizing and taking advantage of informal educational settings to enrich the curricula and help students develop an awareness and sense of responsibility for the world around them. Whether exploring the environment, fostering literacy, enhancing appreciation of the arts, or studying the realms of the sciences, teachers can draw upon a roster of educational specialists in parks, acquaria, libraries, museums, and laboratories. Research indicates that student learning in core subjects is enhanced by engagement in programs of environmental education. Key skills in social studies, art, science, and language are utilized to study, document, and understand environmental themes. Nonformal settings provide opportunities for students to see connections between the curricula they are studying and their environment.

There is no subject more accessible, interesting, or important to children than their own natural world. They are detectives, collectors, guardians, and keepers of the world around them, and every tree, rock, blade of grass, bird, squirrel, star, raindrop, and snowflake is an element of joy and wonder. Children are natural observers and constructors of knowledge and the role of teachers is to use these characteristics to create dynamic teaching and learning occasions for their students.

Such settings also provide teaching and learning opportunities for preservice and inservice teachers to become knowledgeable about environmental issues and resources. At New York University, for example, the Wallerstein Collaborative for Urban Environmental Education (EE), in conjunction with other organizations, offers field experiences, courses, internships, seminars, conferences, and workshops to assist teachers in infusing EE content into their curricula (http://www.nyu.edu/wallerstein).

Where Are We Now? Where Are We Headed?

As educators, we find ourselves looking in many directions, still learning from the past and studying the present while looking to the future. American education struggles to be responsive to a multitude of social, economic, and political needs and pressures. As times changed, generation after generation endeavored to find the magic formula for student success. What we have learned is that there is no formula and that we must commit ourselves to a continuing process of inquiry, experimentation, critical analysis, reflection, and perhaps some fantasizing. As Cremin wrote (1966):

In the last analysis, what schooling is uniquely able to do, given the range of agencies that educate, is to make youngsters aware of the constant bombardment of facts, opinions, and values to which they are subjected; to help them question what they see and hear; and, ultimately to give them the intellectual resources they need to make judgments and assess significance. (Cremin, pp. 22–23)

At the same time, we must both welcome change and be prepared to help others adapt to change. "The illiterate of the 21st century will not be those who cannot read and write, but those who cannot learn, unlearn, and relearn" (attributed to Alvin Toffler).

The Ripple Effect

We hope that your initial inquiries into teaching and learning have created a ripple effect, expanding your circles of awareness so that you want to know more about learners and learning, teachers and classrooms, curriculum and assessment, and schools and communities. One of our concerns has been that introductory texts and courses stand apart from the rest of a student's program of study. In this final chapter, therefore, we aim to ensure that you have a sense of what lies ahead for you and that you can make connections between this introductory exploration and ensuing experiences where you will be able to pursue questions in greater depth and simultaneously create new ones.

The Struggles and the Possibilities

We have not hesitated in each of the preceding chapters to point out major strengths and weaknesses in the educational system. Here we give prominence to several permeating problems while also sharing our perceptions of some positive signs. Most of the problems are not new, but the sporadic efforts to deal with them to date have accomplished little. Unless we—teachers, administrators, parents, and teacher educators—have the courage and the commitment to deal with these matters in an ongoing and concerted manner, we will fail the students for whom we say schooling is dedicated.

Families and Schools

The relationship between parents or guardians and teachers is often described as ambiguous. Across cultural and social class lines, at its best it is mutually supportive, but at its worst, it is contentious. Parents want their children to succeed and try to respect and cooperate with their children's teachers, but at times they meet barriers of impatience, distrust, and limited communication. Teachers want their students to succeed and would like the support of parents, but at times feel threatened and frustrated by parental resistance and school bureaucracy. Frequently neither parents nor teachers understand each other's intentions, and as in most such relationships there are occasions of misunderstanding and mutual distrust. Nevertheless, these partnerships are a decisive factor in student performance.

In many suburban, small town, and rural communities, parents often have access to interact with their children's teachers, school administrators, and school boards. For one thing, parents have the clout that comes with the power of the purse and many have learned to work the system. They can use the ballot box to approve or reject the school budget. Their participation on school boards, in the local PTAs, and in various school activities gives them additional visibility. Competitive school sports are often community events; parents are involved because their children are involved, but often attend merely as spectators to support their community's teams.

Unfortunately even this kind of superficial involvement does not pertain in large cities for parents who are distanced, physically and psychologically, from the schools their children attend. Students with disabilities are often bussed and schooled far from where they live, compounding the limitations of parent–teacher interactions. In many families both parents work; in other families language barriers preclude effective communication. Suspicion and antagonism also arise when parents see schools as places where their religious or cultural values are not respected.

Undoubtedly the most successful model of collaboration among parents, educators, and a local community is the Comer School Development Program at Yale University, created almost 40 years ago by its now internationally acclaimed director, James P. Comer (1980/1993). His intervention program, designed to improve the social, emotional, and academic outcomes of children from low-income families, breaks the cycle of distrust and defensiveness felt by those on both sides of the equation. It includes community leaders and professionals from social and medical agencies who become active members of the school environment. The result is a working climate of shared power. Comer's program offers excellent examples of approaches that have proven successful in hundreds of communities where they have been adapted. Home–school partnerships, as Susan McAllister Swap (1993) confirms, are not solely the responsibility of parents and teachers; they must be seen in the contexts of school/community cultures and district, state, and federal policies (p. xiii).

Strange as it may seem, the tendency is for greater success at collaboration between the parents and teachers of early childhood, elementary, and special education children than between parents and teachers of adolescents. At the stages of preadolescence and adolescence, youngsters struggle with drastic physical changes, crucial personal and intellectual dilemmas, and incessant social and academic pressures. This is the period when they most need the consistency, caring, understanding, and support of parents and teachers; too often this is the time when they receive the least. Why is this so? There are several possible reasons:

Parents, unable to communicate with their teenage sons and daughters and/or failing to establish clear norms for their adolescents' behaviors, opt out and delegate responsibility to teachers.

Racial and cultural traditions and language barriers prevent effective collaboration between parents and teachers.

Parents feel inadequate about their knowledge of the subject content their children are studying.

Secondary school teachers, overburdened by several large classes daily and somewhat doubtful of the role parents are playing in their children's lives, resist entering into joint efforts.

Departmentalized school curricula in secondary schools discourage parents who find that they have to relate to several different teachers.

Teachers with high enrollments in their classes have only limited knowledge of each of their students.

Students prefer to keep their home and school lives separate and go to great lengths to prevent their parents and teachers from making contacts with each other.

The explanations are multiple. Psychologists talk of generation gaps, of students' ambivalence toward emancipation from home, of strong peer group influences, of the powerful draw of outside forces. Sociologists point to social class differences between parents and teachers. Teachers worry about student alienation and parental resistance, in addition to coping with the expectations of the accountability system imposed upon them. Administrators are discouraged in spite of their experiments with strategies to enlist parents' participation. Whatever the reasons, genuine collaboration between parents and secondary school personnel, though badly needed, is sorely lacking.

Teachers and families must see their roles as a continuous process that begins in early childhood and extends through the educational continuum. Just as there are transition programs for students as they move from one level of schooling to another, similar programs should exist for parents as well. And, teachers must learn to understand the needs and values of the school's community and work with parents to develop strategies that support children at home.

Inequality and Diversity

For a nation recognized as a model of democracy, it is hard to believe how profoundly inequality pervades our society. As an expression of deeply embedded attitudes toward difference, inequality is most visible in our urban centers in the treatment of people of color and of low socioeconomic status, but it is subliminally diffused throughout our communities, schools, workplaces, and cultural institutions. It affects large numbers of children and youth who are different because they are girls or boys, or are identified by particular abilities or disabilities, the primary language they speak, the country of origin they identify with, the religious beliefs they hold, or the sexual orientation they choose. Whether one sees difference through the lens of stereotype, prejudice, ignorance, or fear, the impact of inequality remains a devastating and destructive force.

Pedro Noguera (2003), a strong advocate on behalf of poor children and children of color, does not mince words:

> As long as we are able to convince ourselves that simply providing access to education is equivalent to providing equal opportunity, we will continue to treat failing schools as a nonissue. We will also continue to delude ourselves with the notion that the United States is a democracy based on genuine meritocratic principles: a society where social mobility is determined by individual talent and effort. We hold on to this fantasy even as a quarter of the nation's children are denied adequate educational opportunity. (p.15)

Many urban schools suffer from an imbalance of equity. Certain districts receive more funding than others, creating a have-and-have-not system. Savvy parents are able to negotiate for resources and programs for their students, whereas poorer, less sophisticated parents who do not know the ropes are powerless to do the same. Noguera questions how this situation can possibly be sanctioned:

> The fact that the United States tolerates the failure of so many of its urban schools suggests that there is either a pervasive belief that poor children are not entitled to anything better or an active conspiracy to ensure that the majority of children who are born poor, stay poor. (Noguera, 2003, pp. 15–16)

From our perspective, this statement applies not only to the poor, but to all the disenfranchised populations of students who have diverse and special needs.

No one claims that discriminatory behavior lends itself to a quick fix or that teachers alone should be expected to assume this awesome responsibility, but educators especially cannot assume an ostrich-like stance. At the least, we must ensure that throughout the school environment, equality and genuine respect for all students and their families are enforced.

Leadership

Leadership is commonly described as a process through which an individual influences others to achieve objectives. We need educational leaders at various levels in our schools and communities, in our professional associations, and in our legislative, executive, and judicial branches of government. In this section, we focus on three groups: teachers, principals, and politicians.

Of all the groups who should enact leadership, teachers have been the least likely to be recognized as leaders. Most unheralded are the teacher leaders who, along with their daily teaching, mentor younger colleagues, serve as models, advocate for students, write proposals to seek funding, assume responsibility as union representatives, and take on the multitude of activities that enhance the work of their colleagues. Sadly teachers making headlines are usually those who have acted inappropriately.

John G. Gabriel (2005) categorizes teacher leadership in four areas: influencing school culture, building and maintaining a successful team, equipping other potential leaders, and enhancing or improving student achievement. Unfortunately, too many teachers are bogged down by the clerical demands of their classrooms or are uninterested in taking on an additional role. As a result, they often allow other school personnel to assume the responsibilities that they could most appropriately handle. Gabriel makes the case clear: "Inviting teachers to participate in the decision-making process by elevating them to leadership roles should be viewed as a means to accomplish significant change in the field of education" (p. 156).

In a policy brief, "Effective Leaders for Today's Schools" (1999), produced by a Policy Forum on Educational Leadership, 40 leading experts discussed definitions of leadership, successful practices, professional development needs, and the research and policy implications of new ways of thinking about leadership. Their report addressed issues appropriate to both school superintendents and principals. They defined effective leadership for today's schools under four headings: (1) instructional leadership, (2) management skills, (3) communication, collaboration, and community building, and (4) vision, risk, and change. Drawing on data from case studies, they described instructional leaders as having "a deep understanding of teaching and learning, including new teaching methods that emphasize problem solving and student construction of knowledge," "a strong commitment to success for all students," and a commitment "to improving instruction for groups of students who are not learning now" (p. 1).

As you will discover, in most cases, teachers view their building principals as their primary leader. Regrettably, too many principals are inundated with meetings, reports, maintenance, and public relations events to enact the role most essential to successful teaching and learning. These ongoing administrative tasks leave them with little time to attend to the important work of curriculum and instruction, participating in classrooms, or promoting relevant staff development. When principals were surveyed (*Education Week,* September 15, 2004, p. 57) they reported that the overwhelming portion of their time is devoted to maintaining the physical security of students, faculty, and staff and to managing school facilities, resources, and procedures, with very little time for building a school community, guiding the development of curriculum and evaluation, or engaging staff in professional development activities. Joanne Rooney (2003) makes clear what should really matter:

> Good principals model care. Their words and behavior explicitly show that caring is not optional. Nothing can substitute for this leadership. . . . No principal can ask any teacher, student or parent to travel down the uncertain path of caring if the principal will not lead the way. (p. 76)

Jeff Archer (2004) describes an administrative model with great potential. By introducing the position of "school manager," principals can be freed of administrative duties and enabled to focus on being the much-needed instructional leader. We would add, as illustrated by work in this area by Nel Noddings (1992), that caring principals and caring teachers create caring students.

We cannot address all the categories of leaders, but we will not neglect to mention political leaders. Our concerns are several, including that elected officials are rarely knowledgeable about the complexity of teaching and learning, that they have not weighed the impact of the limited financial resources they allocate, and that they have not faced up to the obligations and demands of the growing diversity among the students in our schools. In a penetrating analysis, Seymour Sarason (1998) warns:

> When it comes to school change, we should cease regarding our political leaders as exempt from criticism, as if there are more important things for them to think about. There are no more important things. What happens to our schools (especially urban ones) over the next two decades will be fateful for this country. (p. 139)

Therefore, our concerns about leadership are evident in our schools but go far beyond the schoolroom door. From Washington, D.C. to Main Street, U.S.A., elected officials, policymakers, social action groups, and all citizens—but especially teachers—must commit themselves to gaining an understanding of the complexities of the educational process and use their voices and their designated roles to support education.

Testing

Though previously discussed, we would be remiss here not to identify the obsession with testing as one of the most serious problems plaguing students' and teachers' school experiences. We maintain that rich curricula and differentiated instruction are severely hampered by the overarching attention to "test prep" to the neglect of the individual needs and interests of children and youth.

With standardized testing so pervasive, and so strongly embedded in the law of the land, we cannot expect teachers to subvert the requirements imposed upon them. The best we can hope for, as a temporary measure, is that a reassuring and calming climate can be created in schools and classrooms to reduce the competition, anxiety, labeling, mislabeling, and segregation that these tests engender.

The real challenge facing the profession is to commit itself to building a database that gives evidence from multiple sources that students are learning and growing. Arguing against the tide will not suffice until we can document achievement and success through a variety of alternative means.

Teaching and Learning as an Ethical Enterprise

In preceding sections we raise concerns about several issues with serious implications not only for children and youth but also for the well-being of our democratic society. Education, our society's primary social institution, cannot be neutral; it is an ethical endeavor. The ethical aspects of teaching and learning involve modeling concepts of caring, justice, fairness, equity, of improving the human condition, and protecting our environment. Whether we are teaching biology or literature, geography or music, an ethical stance must pervade.

When Vivian Gussin Paley (1992) in her kindergarten class insists on the rule, "you can't say you can't play," she is assuming an ethical position. Educators and parents can also find opportunities to raise questions and model an ethical stance. When young children read and study traditional fairy tales, do discussions ensue about good and evil, right and wrong, and are similar versions of these tales from other cultures introduced to them as well? When older students engage in competitive sports, will they play fairly and ensure that all teammates get to participate in the game? Will teachers and their students apply the ethics of choice in selecting what to read or will censorship rear its ugly head? Ethical issues remain the same from childhood to adulthood. The real standards schools should promote and measure are how students and teachers embody honesty, integrity, responsibility, respect, and equity in their actions.

Ethical standards should not be confused with religious doctrine, although they may be related. The ethical principles we espouse are inherent in our democratic way of life and must be enacted by teachers and learners in all educational environments. The problems we raise in this section illustrate the subversion of ethical principles in school communities. When schools are ethical enterprises, the voices of parents will be heard, schools will actively attend to the needs of all children, teaching and learning will honor the differences among learners, and educational leaders will assume responsibility for the fulfillment of these commitments.

Looking Ahead

Yet, we have hope! New voices are being heard. The general public and representatives of private industry are beginning to join parents and professional educators in arguing that the "old ways" will not suffice in the new millennium. These are the people who understand that schools must meet the needs of the 21st century. The future depends on individuals with critical and divergent thinking skills who will raise questions, seek alternative solutions to critical problems, and develop and maintain the latest technologies.

We are encouraged by the emergence of numerous public service groups, the creation of Internet sites, and the increased use of petitions, letter writing campaigns, and public forums to express concerns and press for focused attention on the problems and needs of public education.

The most powerful tool is the election process at the local, state, and federal levels, but there are other avenues as well.

Though the major brunt of school financing is born by local, state, and federal taxes, individual philanthropists, often through their foundations, are investing heavily in educational programs to encourage innovations in school reform and support low-income and culturally marginalized children. One example, as reported by *Education Week* (June 16, 2004, pp. 1, 28–30) and in other major publications, is the $2.2 billion in education-related grants made by the Bill and Melinda Gates Foundation for special programs across the country, most particularly for the small schools movement.

Individual contributors are providing motivation and financial assistance to enable children in low socioeconomic communities to pursue higher education. For example, tennis star Andre Agassi supports a charter school and billionaire George Soros has provided numerous educational grants for school and after-school programs. Scholarships are commonly earmarked for special groups while other organizations offer grants and internships for research or development in particular fields of study. Not all of these efforts are well publicized, but they do make a difference.

Fund raising initiatives are also providing opportunities for smaller donations. Among the most creative of these initiatives is Charles Best's nonprofit Internet idea, Donors Choice. Teachers post their proposals for financing classroom needs and contributors earmark their contributions (*New York Times,* December 24, 2003). This interactive arrangement has led to almost 1 million dollars in small grants.

Volunteerism is another form by which private citizens, parents, and college students are lending their support. They contribute their time as tutors, teacher aids, and mentors in classrooms and in after-school programs. The never ending cake sales, raffles, auctions, and fairs provide the chance for people of all generations in all communities to play a role in helping children and teachers.

Most of all, we take heart from the dynamic, well-educated, socially motivated younger and older adults who are entering the ranks of the teaching profession. They include career changers, mothers with grown children, recent liberal arts graduates, immigrants, and veterans of the armed services. If we can make schools welcoming places, these teachers will remain and gradually become a new and energetic corps of educational leaders.

What Comes Next for the Prospective Teacher?

Though many of you may be asking the questions, "How do I get started? What should I do first?" we are suggesting that there are other questions you might consider. We see these questions as falling into widening and overlapping circles, ranging from the practical and immediate to the reflective and continuous. Here are a few questions that might be on your list:

- What strategies can I use to achieve mindful learning in my teaching?
- How can I use exploratory talk and group processes to enhance teaching and learning in my classroom?
- What methods can I use to observe my students while I am teaching a class?
- How do I analyze what I see and how do I apply my findings?
- How do I find out about the individual backgrounds of my students?
- What technology is available in my school and classroom?
- What approaches would enable me to collaborate successfully with colleagues and with the parents and caretakers of my students?
- What methods can I use to develop and assess my own growth as a teacher?

Below are some of the areas that you are likely to study in-depth in subsequent courses:

Human development

Literacy development

Curriculum development

Instructional approaches

Multiculturalism

Socio-political contexts of schooling

Content knowledge

Assessment and evaluation

Technology

As you look ahead, prepare yourself and ask:

What do I know about each of these areas? What more do I want to know? How might my subsequent studies help me to develop the understandings and the skills to answer my questions?

Corresponding to your courses, we hope you will engage in a variety of field-based experiences in different types of schools and communities, in formal and nonformal settings, with learners of different ages and backgrounds. Such varied settings provide the opportunity to observe and work with diverse groups of professionals. Each setting has the potential to expand your understanding of how educators in different positions see their roles and responsibilities, and on what bases they make their decisions about teaching and learning. Each of them can contribute a great deal to enlarging your scope.

If you have entered into a teacher education program, at some stage you will take on the role of a student teacher. You will work with cooperating classroom teachers, as well as with representatives from the university, often referred to as "field advisors," who will periodically visit your class, observe your teaching, conference with you, and discuss your progress. At the same time, you will meet with your peers and with university professors in courses and seminars related to your field assignments. In each of these situations you will interact with people whose insights and expertise can be of tremendous value to you. In essence, you will have not one, but several mentors. It is your chance to raise questions, invite critique, and weigh advice in nonjudgmental, supportive contexts.

Toward Further Inquiry: One More Checklist

We conclude by offering a checklist of suggestions to support and extend your continuing inquiries.

- Join up! Investigate the professional associations in your field and join one that seems most relevant to your interests. Student membership usually requires a very minimal fee, but there are many advantages including learning about the current issues, participating in meetings, and identifying new publications in your field.
- Weigh in! Explore the pros and cons of union affiliation.
- Subscribe! In many cases, membership in a professional association will include a subscription to one of the organization's periodicals. If you choose not to join an association, you should consider subscribing to one of the many professional journals available to you as a way to keep yourself up-to-date and connected with colleagues beyond your immediate location.
- Make connections! As you continue your studies, try not to see your experiences, courses, and field assignments as discrete entities. Seek to make connections among them and with your initial inquiries.
- Find a mentor! Both beginning and experienced teachers benefit from having a trusting relationship with a colleague.
- Talk and listen! Reach out to learners, parents, teachers, peers, supervisors, and professors to capture their beliefs about teaching and learning. Then, weigh what you learn, reject what you cannot accept, and integrate others' views into your own.
- Go online! Via the Internet, find chat rooms that address teachers' concerns. Join one, follow along, and participate in professional conversations.
- Keep up! Read daily newspapers and news magazines. Education is making history every day.

- Save! Cut, clip, and file articles, pictures, stories, reports, artifacts, and other items to enrich your teaching and your students' learning. Don't underestimate how many of these will come in handy.

- Write! Set aside a little time to maintain a learning journal. Even short entries can lend themselves to expanding and refining your beliefs, understandings, questions, and concerns.

- Think ahead! Retain critical items you have produced during your course of study for inclusion in a portfolio you may want to present to prospective employers.

- Network! Build relationships to support your work by keeping in touch with peers, mentors, and professors.

- Believe in yourself and be proud! You have chosen a worthy profession that enriches and improves the lives of others and will continue to do the same for yours.

With education causing a strong ripple effect as an increasingly dominant factor in the social, economic, political, and technological fabric of society, we are confident that the need for teachers is not going out of style. As teachers continue to teach, model, and promote democratic principles, they continue to create the opportunities for all students to reach and fulfill their potential. Although you may have opened this book with preconceived notions, we hope that as you close it you are rethinking your assumptions, refining your educational philosophy, and preparing for the complexity, challenge, unpredictability, excitement, and joy that await you.

Standardized tests also have become widespread in teacher certification systems. Although state regulatory agencies have imposed stringent standards on the colleges and universities that offer teacher education programs, students who are about to graduate from these institutions must also achieve satisfactory results on state-mandated examinations in order to obtain their teaching certificates. Some states use the National Teacher Examination while other states have created their own tests. And, in a few states, periodic testing of inservice teachers is also required.

REFERENCES

A plague for the young homeless. (2004, March 3). *New York Times,* A18.

Archer, J. (2004, September 14). Tackling an impossible job. *Education Week,* S3–S10.

Ayers, W. (1993). *To teach.* New York: Teachers College Press.

Barnes, D. (1992, 1975). *From communication to curriculum* (2nd ed.). Portsmouth, NH: Boynton/Cook.

Barnes, D. (1993). Supporting exploratory talk for learning. In K. M. Pierce & J. Gilles (Eds.), *Cycles of meaning: Exploring the potential of talk in learning.* Portsmouth, NH: Heinemann.

Belkin, L. (2004, September 12). The lessons of classroom 506. *The New York Times Magazine,* 40–49, 62, 104, 110.

Bellack, A. A. (1965). "What knowledge is of most worth?" *The High School Journal, 48,* 318–322.

Bierlein, L. A. (1997). The charter school movement. In D. Ravitch & J. P. Viteritti (Eds.), *New schools for a new century: The redesign for urban education* (pp. 37–60). New Haven: Yale University Press.

Bode, B. H. (1950). *Democracy as a way of life.* New York: Macmillan.

Boomer, G. (1992). Negotiating the curriculum. In G. Boomer, N. Lester, L. C. Onore, & J. Cook (Eds.), *Negotiating the curriculum: Educating for the 21st Century* (pp. 4–14). London: The Falmer Press.

Bransford, J., Derry, S., Berliner, D., Hammerness, K. (with Beckett, K. L.). (2005). Theories of learning and their roles in teaching. In L. Darling-Hammond & J. Bransford (Eds.), *Preparing teachers for a changing world* (pp. 40–87). San Francisco: Jossey-Bass.

Britton, J. (1982). Shaping at the point of utterance. In G. M. Pradl (Ed.), *Prospect and retrospect: Selected essays of James Britton* (pp. 139–145). Montclair, NJ: Boynton-Cook.

Britzman, D. P. (1991). *Practice makes practice: A critical study of learning to teach.* Albany: State University of New York Press.

Brooks, J. G., & Brooks, M. G. (1993). *The case for the constructivist classroom.* Alexandria, VA: Association for Supervision and Curriculum Development.

Bruner, J. (1960). *The process of education.* Cambridge: Harvard University Press.

Bruner, J. (1973). *Beyond the information given: Studies in the psychology of knowing* (pp. 397–425). (J. M. Anglin, Ed.). New York: W. W. Norton & Company.

Bruner, J. (1990). *Acts of meaning.* Cambridge: Harvard University Press.

Burnaford, G., Fischer, J., & Hobson, D. (2001). *Teachers doing research: The power of action through inquiry.* (3rd ed.). Mahwah, NJ: Lawrence Erlbaum Associates.

Campbell, D. M., Cigneti, P. B., Melenyzer, B. J., Nettles, D. H., & Wyman, R. (2001). *How to develop a professional portfolio: A manual for teachers.* Boston: Allyn and Bacon.

Christian, S. (1997). *Exchanging lives: Middle school writers online.* Urbana: National Council of Teachers of English.

Cochran-Smith, M., & Lytle, S. L. (1993). *Inside outside: Teacher research and knowledge.* New York: Teachers College Press.

Cochran-Smith, M. (1995). Uncertain allies: Understanding the boundaries of race and teaching. *Harvard Educational Review, 65*(3), pp. 541–570

Comer, J. P. (1980/1993). *School power: Implications of an intervention project.* New York: The Free Press.

Conant, J. B. (1959). *The American high school today.* New York: McGraw-Hill.

Conant, J. B. (1967). *The comprehensive high school: A second report to interested citizens.* New York: McGraw-Hill.

Cremin, L. A. (1964). *The transformation of the school: Progressivism in American education, 1876–1957.* New York: Vintage Books.

Cremin, L. A. (1966). *The genius of American education.* New York: Vintage Books.

Cremin, L. A. (1988). *American education: The metropolitan experience, 1876–1980.* New York: Harper and Row.

Cross, W. E., Jr. (1971). The Negro to black conversion experience: Toward a psychology of black liberation. *Black World, 20*(9), 13–27.

Cross, W. E., Jr. (1991). *Shades of black: Diversity in African-American identity.* Philadelphia: Temple University Press.

Cross, W. E. Jr. (1978). The Cross and Thomas models of psychological nigrescence. *Journal of Black Psychology, 5*(1), 13–19.

Cubberly. E. P. (1919, 1934). *Public education in the United States: A study and interpretation of American educational history.* (Rev. ed.). Boston: Houghton Mifflin.

Darling-Hammond, L., & Cobb, V. L. (1996). The changing context of teacher education. In F. B. Murray (Ed.), *The teacher educator's handbook: Building a knowledge base for the preparation of teachers* (pp. 14–62). San Francisco: Jossey-Bass.

Darling-Hammond, L., & Bransford, J. (Eds.). (2005). *Preparing teachers for a changing world.* San Francisco: Jossey-Bass.

Davis, C., & Davis, J. (2005). Using technology to create a sense of community. *English Journal, 94,* 36–41.

Delpit, L. (1995). *Other people's children: Cultural conflict in the classroom.* New York: The New Press.

Dewey, J. (1904). *The relation of theory to practice in education: The third NSSE yearbook. (Part 1).* Chicago: University of Chicago Press.

Dewey, J. (1929). *Democracy and education.* New York: Macmillan.

Dewey, J. (1990/1900/1902). *The school and society; The child and the curriculum.* Expanded edition. Chicago: University of Chicago Press.

Dewey, J. (1910/1997). *How we think.* Mineola, New York: Dover Publications, Inc.

Dewey, J. (1897, January). My pedagogic creed. *The School Journal,* 54(3), 77–80.

Diamond, C. T. P. (1995). Education and the narrative self: Of maps and stories. *Advances in Personal Construct Psychology, 3,* 79–100.

Duckworth, E. (1991). *"The having of wonderful ideas" and other essays on teaching and learning.* New York: Teachers College Press.

Education Commission of the States. (1983). *A summary of major reports on education.* Denver: The Commission.

Education Week Research Center. (2004, September 15). Instructional leadership. *Education Week, S7.*

Elbow, P. (1973). *Writing without teachers.* Oxford: Oxford University Press.

Ely, M. (with Anzul, M., Friedman, T., Garner, D., & Steinmetz, A. M.). (1991). *Doing qualitative research: Circles within circles.* Bristol, PA: The Falmer Press.

Feiman-Nemser, S., & Buchman, M. (1985). Pitfalls of experience in teacher education. *Teachers College Record, 87,* 53–65.

Ferguson, D. (1996). Is it inclusion yet? Bursting the bubbles. In M. S. Berres, D. L. Ferguson, P. Knoblock, & C. Woods (Eds.), *Creating tomorrow's school today: Stories of inclusion, change, and renewal* (pp. 16–37). New York: Teachers College Press.

Fosnot, C. T. (1989). *Enquiring teachers, enquiring learners: A constructivist approach for teaching.* New York: Teachers College Press.

Fosnot, C. T. (Ed.). (1996). *Constructivism: Theory, perspectives, and practice.* New York: Teachers College Press.

Fraser, J. W. (2001). *The school in the United States: A documentary history.* New York: McGraw-Hill.

Freire, P. (1970). *Pedagogy of the oppressed.* New York: Continuum.

Fullan, M. (1993). *Change forces: Probing the depths of educational reform.* New York: The Falmer Press.

Gabriel, J. G. (2005). *How to thrive as a teacher leader.* Alexandria, VA: Association for Supervision and Curriculum Development.

Gardner, H. (1985). *Frames of mind: The theory of multiple intelligences.* New York: Basic Books.

Gates, H. L., Jr. (2004, August 1). Breaking the silence [op. ed.]. *The New York Times,* p. 11.

Gilyard, K. (1991). *Voices of the self: A study of language competence.* Detroit: Wayne State University Press.

Gilyard, K. (1993). Language learning and democratic development. *Twelve Pages, 2*(3), 3–8.

Giroux, H. A. (1988). *Teachers as intellectuals: Toward a critical pedagogy of learning.* Granby, MA: Bergin & Garvey.

Goldstone, L. (2000). The mother tongue. In *What Matters Most: Improving Student Achievement.* The Teachers Network: IMPACT II.

Good, T. L., & Braden, J. S. (2000). Charter schools: Another reform failure or a worthwhile investment. *Kappan, 81*(10), 721–725.

Goswami, D., & Stillman, P. E. (1987). *Reclaiming the classroom: Teacher research as an agency of change.* Portsmouth, NH: Boynton/Cook.

Griesemer, J., & Butler, C. (1983). *Education under fire: An analysis of recent major reports on education.* Chelmsford, MA: The Northeast Regional Exchange, Inc.

Grumet, M. R. (1989). Generations: Reconceptualist curriculum theory and teacher education. *Journal of Teacher Education, 40*(17), 13–17.

Helms, J. E. (Ed.). (1990). Black and white racial identity: Theory, research and practice. Westport, CT: Greenwood Press.

Hendrie, C. (2004, June 16). High schools nationwide paring down. *Education Week,* pp. 1, 28–30.

Heward, W. L., & Cavanaugh, R. P. (1993). Educational equality for students with disabilities. In J. A. Banks and C. A. M. Banks (Eds.), *Multicultural education: Issues and perspectives* (2nd ed., pp. 237–278). Boston: Allyn and Bacon.

Hirsch, E. D. Jr. (1988). *Cultural literacy: What every American needs to know.* New York: Houghton Mifflin.

Hirsch, E. D. Jr. (1996). *The schools we need: Why we don't have them.* New York: Doubleday.

Jackson, P. W. (1968). *Life in classrooms.* New York: Holt, Rinehart and Winston.

Jeub, C. (1994). Why parents choose home schooling. *Educational Leadership, 52*(1), 50–52.

Karp, S. (2003). Drive-by school reform. In L. Christensen & S. Karp (Eds.), *Rethinking school reform: Views from the classroom.* Milwaukee: Rethinking Schools.

Kelso, E. B. (2005). Middle school students engaging in literacy discussions online. Unpublished doctoral dissertation, New York University, Steinhardt School of Education, New York.

Kincheloe, J. L., & Pinar, W. (Eds.). (1991). *Curriculum as social psychoanalysis: The significance of place.* Albany: State University of New York Press.

Kirp, D. L. (2005, July 31). All my children. *The New York Times,* Education Life, pp. 20–22.

Kirschenbaum, H., Simon, S. B., & Napier, R. W. (1971). *Wad-ja-get? The grading game in American education.* New York: Hart.

Klonsky, M. (1995). *Small schools: The numbers tell the story.* Chicago: UIC Publication Services.

Kohn, A. (1999). *The schools our children deserve: Moving beyond traditional classrooms and "tougher standards."* New York: Houghton Mifflin.

Kohn, A. (2000). *The case against standardized testing: Raising the scores, ruining the schools.* Portsmouth, NH: Heinemann.

Kotulak, R. (2004). Scientists offer hope for poor readers. *Chicago Tribune Online Edition.* Retrieved May 02, 2004, from www. chicagotribune.com/news/local/ chi-0405020482may02,1,4018114.story.

Kozol, J. (1991). *Savage inequalities: Children in America's schools.* New York: Crown.

Ladson-Billings, G. (1994). *The dreamkeepers: Successful teachers of African American children.* San Francisco: Jossey-Bass.

Lakoff, G., & Johnson, M. (1980; 2003). *Metaphors we live by.* Chicago: University of Chicago Press.

Langer, E. J. (1997). *The power of mindful learning.* Reading, MA: Perseus Books.

Larabee, D. F. (2005). Life on the margins. *Journal of Teacher Education, 56*(3), 189.

Lawrence-Lightfoot, S., & Davis, J. H. (1997). *The art and science of portraiture.* San Francisco: Jossey-Bass.

Lightfoot, S. L. (1983). *The good high school: Portraits of character and culture.* New York: Basic Books.

Lines, P. M. (1995). Home schooling comes of age. *Educational Leadership, 53*(2), 63–66.

Lortie, D. (1975). *Schoolteacher: A sociological study.* Chicago: University of Chicago Press.

Major Gates foundation grants to support small high schools. (2004, June 16). *Education Week,* 28–29.

Manno, B. V., Finn, C. E., & Vanourek, G. (2000). Beyond the schoolhouse door: How are charter schools transforming U.S. public education? *Kappan, 81*(10), 736–744.

Mayher, J. S. (1990). *Uncommon sense: Theoretical practice in language education.* Portsmouth, NH: Boynton/Cook.

Mayher, J. S. (1999). Reflections on standards and standard setting: An insider/outside perspective on the NCTE/IRA standards. *English Education, 31*(2), 106–121.

McDonald, J. P. (1992). *Teaching: Making sense of an uncertain craft.* New York: Teachers College Press.

McDonald, J. P. (1996). *Redesigning school: Lessons for the 21st century.* San Francisco: Jossey-Bass.

McIntosh, P. (1988). White privilege and male privilege: A personal account of coming to see correspondences through work in women's studies. A working paper. Wellesley, MA: Wellesley College Center for Research on Women.

McIntosh, P. (1989, July/August). White privilege: Unpacking the knapsack. *Peace and Freedom,* pp.10–12.

McLaren, P. (1989). *Life in schools: An introduction to critical pedagogy in the foundations of education.* New York: Longman.

McNeil, L. M. (1986). *Contradictions of control: School structure and school knowledge.* New York: Routledge.

McNeil, L. M. (2000). *Contradictions of school reform: Educational costs of standardized tests.* New York: Routledge.

Meier, D. (1995). *The power of their ideas: Lessons for America from a small school in Harlem.* Boston: Beacon Press.

Meyer, A. E. (1965). *An educational history of the Western world.* New York: McGraw-Hill.

Miner, B. (2003). For-profits target education. In L. Christensen & S. Karp (Eds.), *Rethinking school reform: Views from the classroom.* Milwaukee: Rethinking Schools.

Minnich, E. K. (1990). *Transforming knowledge.* Philadelphia: Temple University Press.

National Commission on Excellence in Education. (1984). *A nation at risk: The full account.* Portland, OR: USA Research, Inc.

National Commission on Teaching and America's Future. (1996). *What matters most: Teaching for America's future.* New York: The Commission.

National Institute on Educational Governance, Finance, Policymaking, and Management, Office of Educational Research and Improvement, Department of Education. (1999). Policy Brief: Effective Leaders for Today's Schools: Synthesis of a Policy Forum on Educational Leadership. Available online at http://www.ed.gov/pubs/EffectiveLeaders/title.html.

National Research Council. (2000). *How people learn: Brain, mind, experience, and school.* Washington, DC: National Academies Press.

Nieto, S. (1999). *The light in their eyes: Creating multicultural learning communities.* New York: Teachers College Press.

Nieto, S. (2000). *Affirming diversity: The sociopolitical context of multicultural education* (3rd ed.). New York: Addison-Wesley.

Nieto, S. (2003). Preface. In L. Christensen & S. Karp (Eds.), *Rethinking school reform: Views from the classroom.* Milwaukee: Rethinking Schools.

Noddings, N. (1992). *The challenge to care in schools: An American approach to education.* New York: Teachers College Press.

Noguera, P. (2003). *City schools and the American dream: Reclaiming the promise of public education.* New York: Teachers College Press.

Ohanian, S. (1999). *One size fits few: The folly of educational standards.* Portsmouth, NH: Heinemann.

Paley, V. G. (1992). *You can't say you can't play.* Cambridge, MA: Harvard University Press.

Palmer, P. J. (1998). *The courage to teach: Exploring the inner landscape of a teacher's life.* San Francisco: Jossey-Bass.

Paris, C. L. (1993). *Teacher agency and curriculum making in classrooms.* New York: Teachers College Press.

Perkins, D. (1992). *Smart schools: Better thinking and learning for every child.* New York: The Free Press.

Perkinson, H. J. (1968). *The imperfect panacea: American faith in education, 1865–1965.* New York: Random House.

Perrone, V. (1999). *Lessons for new teachers.* New York: McGraw Hill.

Piaget, J., & Inhelder, B. (1969). *The psychology of the child.* New York: Basic Books.

Pinar, W. (1995). *Autobiography, politics and sexuality.* New York: Peter Lang.

Pinar, W. (1988). Whole, bright, deep with understanding: Issues in qualitative research and autobiographical method. In W. P. Pinar (Ed.), *Contemporary curriculum discourses* (pp. 134–153). Scottsdale, AZ: Gorsuch Scarisbrick.

Pollack, W. (1998). *Real boys: Rescuing our sons from the myths of boyhood.* New York: Henry Holt.

Popham, W. J. (2001). *The truth about testing: An educator's call to action.* Alexandria, VA: Association for Supervision and Curriculum Development.

Pradl, G. M. (1996). *Literature for democracy: Reading as a social act.* Portsmouth, NH: Boynton/Cook.

Ravitch, D. (2000). *Left back: A century of failed school reform.* New York: Simon & Shuster.

Ravitch, D., & Viteritti, J. P. (1997). *New schools for a new century: The redesign for urban education.* New Haven: Yale University Press.

Ravitch, D. & Finn, C. (1988). *What do our 17 year olds know? A report on the First national assessment of history and literature.* New York: Harper Collins.

Ray, B. D. (2002). Customization through homeschooling. *Educational Leadership, 59*(7), 50–53.

Reich, R. (2002). The civic perils of homeschooling. *Educational Leadership, 59*(7), 56–59.

Resnick, L. B. (1991). Shared cognition: Thinking as social practice. In L. B. Resnick, J. M. Levine, & S. D. Teasley (Eds.), *Perspectives on socially shared cognition* (pp. 1–20). Washington, DC: American Psychological Association.

Rickford, J. R. (1997, December). Suite for ebonics and phonics. *Discover Magazine.* 82–87.

Rooney, J. (2003, March). Principals who care: A personal reflection. *Educational Leadership, 60* (6), 76–78.

Rosenblatt, L. M. (1938/1965). *Literature as exploration.* New York: Noble and Noble.

Rosenblatt, L. M. (1978). *The reader, the text, the poem: The transactional theory of the literary work.* Carbondale, IL: Southern Illinois University Press.

Sacks, P. (1999). *Standardized minds: The high price of America's testing culture and what we can do to change it.* Cambridge, MA: Perseus.

Sadker, M., & Sadker, D. (1994). *Failing at fairness: How America's schools cheat girls.* New York: Charles Scribner's Sons.

Sarason, S. B. (1971). *The culture of the school and the problem of change.* Boston: Allyn & Bacon, Inc.

Sarason, S. B. (1998). *Political leadership and educational failure.* San Francisco: Jossey-Bass.

Schemo, D. J. (2004, August 17). Charter schools trail in results, U.S. data reveals. *The New York Times,* p. A1, A19.

Schön, D. (1983). *The reflective practitioner: How professionals think in action.* New York: Basic Books.

Short, K. G., Schroeder, J., Kauffman, G., & Kaser, S. (2004, May). Thoughts from the editors. *Language Arts, 81*(5), 367.

Sizer, T. R. (1984). *Horace's compromise: The dilemma of the American high school.* Boston: Houghton Mifflin.

Sleeter, C. E., & Grant, C. A. (1999). *Making choices for multicultural education: Five approaches to race, class, and gender* (3rd ed.). New York: John Wiley and Sons.

Sobelman, M. (1996). *Weaving a richly textured course: Developing Inquiries into Teaching and Learning.* [Monograph]. New York: New York University School of Education.

Sobelman, M. (1999). *Weaving a richly textured course: The changing tapestry of Inquiries into Teaching and Learning.* [Monograph]. New York: New York University School of Education.

Sobelman, M., & Krasnow, M. (1998). *Exploring students' beliefs about teaching, learning, and classroom practice: Inquiries into teaching and learning.* Unpublished report. New York: New York University School of Education.

Spencer, H. (1911). *Essays on education etc.* London: J. M. Dent & Sons.

Sprenger, M. (1999). *Learning and memory: The brain in action.* Alexandria, VA: Association for Supervision and Curriculum Development.

Stenhouse, L. (1975). *An introduction to curriculum research and development.* London: Heinemann.

Stibbs, A. (1979). *Assessing children's language.* Sheffield, UK: National Association for the Teaching of English.

Swap, S. M. (1993). *Developing home-school partnerships: From concepts to practice.* New York: Teachers College Press.

Talk Workshop Group. (1982). *Becoming our own experts.* London: ILEA English Centre.

Tatum, B. (1992). Talking about race; learning about racism: The application of racial identity development. *Harvard Educational Review, 62*(1), 1–24.

Themba-Nixon, M. (2003). Choice and other white lies. In L. Christensen & S. Karp (Eds.), *Rethinking school reform: Views from the classroom.* Milwaukee: Rethinking Schools.

Townsend, J. S. (1998.) Silent voices: What happens to quiet students during classroom discussions? *English Journal, 87*(2), 72–80.

Turnbull, A., Turnbull, R., Shank, M., & Leal, D. (1999). *Exceptional lives: Special education in today's schools* (2nd ed.). New Jersey: Prentice-Hall.

Turnbull, R. H., III. (1986). *Free appropriate education: The law and children with disabilities.* Denver, CO: Love.

Tyack, D., & Cuban, L. (1995). *Tinkering with utopia: A century of public school reform.* Cambridge, MA: Harvard University Press.

Verdi, G. G. (2000). Navigating languages and cultures: An ethnographic study of four working-class women academics. Unpublished doctoral dissertation. New York University, Steinhardt School of Education, New York.

Vygotsky, L. (1978). *Mind in society: The development of higher psychological processes.* Cambridge, MA: Harvard University Press.

Wells, G., & Wells, G. L. (1992). *Constructing knowledge together: Classrooms as centers of inquiry and literacy.* Portsmouth, NH: Heinemann.

Whitehead, A. N. (1949). *The aims of education and other essays.* New York: Mentor Books.

Wiggins, G. (1990). The case for authentic assessment. *Practical Assessment, Research & Evaluation.* Available at http://ericae.net/pare/getvn.asp?v=28n-2.

Wiggins, G. (1998). *Educative assessment: Designing assessments to inform and improve student performance.* San Francisco: Jossey-Bass.

Willis, Scott. (2002). Customization and the common good: A conversation with Larry Cuban. *Educational Leadership, 59*(7), 6–11.

Wolfe, P. (2001). *Brain matters: Translating research into classroom practice.* Alexandria, VA: Association for Supervision and Curriculum Development.

Zernike, K. (2001). The Harvard guide to happiness. *The New York Times,* Education Life, pp. 18, 20.

Zessoules, R., & Gardner, H. (1991). Authentic assessment: Beyond the buzzword and into the classroom. In V. Perrone (Ed.), *Expanding student assessment.* Alexandria, VA: Association for Supervision and Curriculum Development.

Zigler, E., & Styfco, S. J. (Eds.). (1993). *Head Start and beyond: A national plan for intervention.* New Haven, CT: Yale University Press.

Appendix

Autobiographies, Memoirs, and Personal Narratives of Teachers and Learners

Ashton-Warner, Sylvia. (1963/1986). *Teacher.* New York: Simon and Schuster.

First published in 1963, *Teacher* is part diary and part inspired description of the author's teaching methods in action. For many years, Ashton-Warner taught Maori children in an "infant room" in a small country school in New Zealand. She devised a revolutionary method called "organic teaching," whereby written words became prized possessions for her students. Her goal was for her children to want to possess learning.

Ayers, William. (1993). *To Teach: The Journey of a Teacher.* New York: Teachers College Press.

Ayers describes education as "bold, adventurous, creative, vivid, illuminating. . . . Education tears down the walls; training is all barbed wire." Jonathan Kozol says: "No one since John Holt has written so thoughtfully about the things that actually happen in the classroom. Ayers has been there and he knows, and he shares what he has learned with tremendous sensitivity . . . [He] writes so beautifully of children he has known . . . that this book will touch the heart of almost anyone who loves the authenticity of oral history."

Cary, Lorene. (1991). *Black Ice.* New York: Vintage Books.

In 1992, Lorene Cary, a bright, ambitious black teenager from Philadelphia, was transplanted into the formerly all-White, all-male environs of the elite Saint Paul's School in New Hampshire, where she became a scholarship student in a "boot camp" for future

American leaders. Like any good student, she was determined to succeed—but to succeed without selling out. This memoir describes the perils and ambiguities of that double role, in which both failing calculus and winning a student election could be interpreted as betrayals of one's skin. *Black Ice* is also a recognizable document of a woman's adolescence; it is, as Houston Baker says, "a journey into selfhood that resonates with sober reflection, intelligent passion, and joyous love."

Fecho, Bob. (2004). *"Is This English?" Race, Language, and Culture in the Classroom.* New York: Teachers College Press.

Bob Fecho tells the inspiring story of his journey as an English teacher who gradually succeeds in using a critical inquiry approach with his alienated and economically, socially, and politically marginalized African-American and Caribbean high school students. Drawing on rich illustrations from his 20 years in the classroom, Fecho explains, "As my theory and practice transact, creating what is known as praxix, I continue to develop my philosophy of teaching and learning." Fecho's recounting of his experiences offers support and encouragement to both novice and veterans teachers.

Frank, Anne. (1996). *Diary of a Young Girl: The Definitive Edition.* New York: Anchor Press.

This new edition of Anne Frank's classic diary captures the youthful exuberance, spirit, and tragedy of an adolescent girl whose words have given testimony to the horrors of the Holocaust. It is a coming of age account of a young woman's courage and sensitivity, written while in hiding in an attic to escape the Gestapo. This text restores entries omitted from the original edition, revealing a new depth to Anne's dreams, irritations, hardships, and passions. Anne emerges as more real, more human, and more vital than ever.

Fricke, Aaron. (1995). *Reflections of a Rock Lobster: A Story About Growing Up Gay.* Los Angeles: Allyson Books.

This book presents a realistic and unglamorized portrayal of the life of a gay teen. Aaron Fricke tackles the world of homophobia, exposing the lies that work as the foundation for many arguments. One of his high school peers wrote: "I am grateful that I knew him then. Only after reading *Reflections of a Rock Lobster* did I realize how difficult it was for him at that time in his life." Another wrote: "I only wish that I had the willpower at that stage of my life to have stood up with him rather than condemn him."

Glover, Mary Kenner. (1997). *Making School by Hand: Developing a Meaning-Centered Curriculum from Everyday Life.* Urbana: NCTE.

In *Making School by Hand,* Mary Kenner Glover reveals how her childhood interests and experiences have deeply influenced what she has created in her own school and classroom. Using the metaphor of a quilt, she shows how teaching can be approached as a "handmade" process, and how we can use the materials of everyday life to develop a curriculum to meet the needs and interests of our students. Glover presents creative classroom activities—such as building models of the human body, designing and playing board games with environmental themes, and bringing books to life through dance performances—that lead to surprises and discoveries.

Grandin, Temple. (1995). *Thinking in Pictures and Other Reports from My Life with Autism.* New York: Vintage Books.

Temple Grandin, Ph.D., is a gifted animal scientist who has designed one-third of all the livestock-handling facilities in the United States. In this unprecedented book, Grandin delivers a report from the country of autism. Writing from the dual perspectives of a scientist and an autistic person, she tells us how that country is experienced by its inhabitants and how she managed to breach its boundaries to function in the outside world. What emerges in *Thinking in Pictures* is the document of an extraordinary human being, one who, in gracefully and lucidly bridging the gulf between her condition and our own, sheds light on the riddle of our common identity.

Hoffman, Eve. (1989). *Lost in Translation: A Life in a New Language.* New York: Penguin.

When her parents brought her from the war-ravaged, faded elegance of her native Cracow in 1959 to settle in well-manicured, suburban Vancouver, Eva Hoffman was 13 years old. Entering into adolescence, she endured the painful pull of nostalgia, suffered in schools where she did not understand others and where no one tried to understand her, and struggled to express herself in a strange, unyielding new language. A chronicle of upward mobility and assimilation, *Lost in Translation* is also an incisive meditation on coming to terms with one's uniqueness, on learning how deeply culture affects the mind and body, and finally, on what it means to accomplish a translation of one's self. A review in *Newsday* said: "Hoffman raises one provocative question after another about the relationship between language and culture . . . and about the emotional cost of re-creating oneself."

Hunter, Latoya. (1992). *The Diary of Latoya Hunter: My First Year in Junior High.* New York: Crown.

Latoya's innermost thoughts are recorded in her diary as events happen. Her experiences during her first year at JHS 80 in the Bronx are described in the simple but luminous prose of an intelligent, sensitive, shy, and deeply feeling young woman. Her school days, her growing independence, her conflicts with her mother, her first love, the violence she sees in her neighborhood, and her visit to her Jamaican birthplace are all part of her unique, affirmative, inspiring, moving, human, and real story.

Hunter-Gault, Charlayne. (1993). *In My Place.* New York: Vintage Books.

On a January morning in 1961, 19-year-old Charlayne Hunter walked calmly into history as she passed through a gauntlet of jeering Whites to become the first Black woman to attend the University of Georgia. With enormous candor and a courage that is all the more extraordinary for insisting on its ordinariness, the award-winning journalist and correspondent for the *MacNeil/Lehrer News Hour* recounts her transformation from a girl who grew up wanting to be Brenda Starr to a young woman who, with quiet confidence, crossed America's racial divide. *In My Place* is a powerful act of witness to the brutal realities of segregation and an homage to the Black culture that prepared Charlayne Hunter-Gault to challenge hatred and transcend it.

Jennings, Kevin, Ed. (1994). *One Teacher in 10: Gay and Lesbian Educators Tell Their Stories.* Boston: Allyson.

Gay and lesbian teachers have traditionally dwelt in the deepest of closets. But increasing numbers of young people are now served by teachers who are out and proud. Here, for the first time, educators from all regions of the country tell about their experiences, their struggles and victories, as they have put their own careers at risk in their fight for justice. *One Teacher in 10* is a collection of powerful and personal stories and a useful introduction to homophobia and homosexuality.

Kingston, Maxine Hong. (1975). *The Woman Warrior: Memoir of a Girlhood Among Ghosts.* New York: Vintage Books.

Somehow, it always goes back to mom—how we, as women, are molded (or unmolded) by the influence of our mothers. Who are we, as women? How have we become products of our culture? What do we run toward? From what do we run away? Why? This fascinating story tells the tales and mysteries of many "women warriors" of Chinese heritage. Through oral histories shared by her mother, our narrator leads us through the lives of the women in her family who grew up in China and migrated to America. There are intriguing and haunting tales of superstition and tradition, yet the storyline of the female struggle for identity and survival in a culture where women barely rate third-class citizenship is poignant and gut wrenching. The conflict of growing up in America, East meeting West, is avidly and painfully portrayed.

Kohl, Herbert. (1967/1988). *36 Children.* New York: Penguin.

This is the remarkable account of an innovative and open-minded young teacher's year with a Harlem sixth-grade class. First published in 1967, Kohl's shocking revelations and insightful solutions to the problems of an urban school shook the foundations of education. He was warned that his students were unmanageable and unteachable, and he saw teachers resort to strict discipline to disguise their fear. Yet as he closely observed and listened to his students, he discovered they were as concerned as he to make the class work. With the atmosphere of trust he created, the classroom became a sanctuary that allowed the students to confront the poverty and violence of their everyday lives and discover the possibilities of a world beyond their immediate environment.

Koshewa, Allen. (1999). *Discipline and Democracy: Teachers on Trial.* Portsmouth: Heinemann.

Allen Koshewa knows from hard-won experience that one needn't abandon democratic ideals when faced with the challenge of a difficult class. He documents it all in this report of his life in a turbulent fifth-grade class where a total breakdown of order occurred. In the foreword, Jerome Harste writes: "From reading this book, new and veteran teachers can learn how to face difficult students without abandoning their most fundamental democratic beliefs and values."

Louganis, Greg. (1996). *Breaking the Surface.* NY: Plume/Penguin.

The author is a champion diver who won back-to-back double gold medals at the 1984 and 1988 Olympics. Yet, throughout his youth and high profile career, he struggled with self-doubts, a lack of confidence, and the anguish of believing he had to conceal his homosexuality. He recounts how he eventually found the strength to come out as an HIV-positive gay man and finally achieved a sense of well being and happiness.

Malcolm X with Alex Haley. (1966). *The Autobiography of Malcolm X.* New York: Grove Press.

This is the absorbing personal story of the man who rose from a life of crime to become a dynamic leader of the civil rights movement. It is, too, a testament of great emotional power from which every American can learn much. Above all, this book shows the Malcolm X that very few people knew—the man behind the stereotyped image of the hate-preacher, a sensitive, proud, highly intelligent man whose plan to move into the mainstream was cut short by a hail of assassins' bullets—a man who felt certain he would not live long enough to see his book appear.

Meier, Deborah. (1995). *The Power of Their Ideas: Lessons for America from a Small School in Harlem.* Boston: Beacon Press.

Deborah Meier was invited 21 years ago by her district superintendent in East Harlem to start a school for students in the neighborhood. Years later, Central Park East is considered one of the most successful and innovative public schools in New York City and serves as a model for the small school movement. In her book, Meier discusses her commitment to public education as part of her commitment to democracy in America and provides many examples from her experience at Central Park East to show how public schools can be reformed to better serve students. Meier is honest about the complexity of schooling and does not claim reform can happen overnight, but her devotion to improved public education is inspiring.

Monette, Paul. (1992). *Becoming a Man: Half a Life Story.* San Francisco: Harper Collins.

This is a book about what it was like for a young man growing up in the 1950s in a small New England town, unable to come to terms with his gay identity, having to keep the secret from himself and from others. It talks about the unhappiness of Monette's years as a boy in an exclusive private school, then in an Ivy League college, and his subsequent rejection of straight privilege on his quest to find himself and to find love. It is a book about celebrating life, and it is a book about death; it discusses the author's struggle with loss and illness and his efforts to add his story to "the tale of the tribe." A reviewer for the *L.A. Weekly* wrote: "One of the most complex, moral, personal and political books to have been written about gay life." Paul Monette died of an AIDS-related illness in 1995.

Peck, Scott. (1995). *All-American Boy: A Memoir.* Los Angeles: Alyson Books.

Scott Peck, destined for a career as a fundamentalist minister, and his father, Marine colonel Fred Peck, were estranged for 14 years while Scott grew up in a sometimes abusive home. Then, a mere five days before he was to testify against allowing gays into the military, Fred Peck learned that his only son is gay. *All-American Boy* is a powerful and personal document and an unforgettable portrait of courage and love.

Perrone, Vito. (1998). *Teacher with a Heart.* New York: Teachers College Press.

Vito Perrone invites you on an inspirational journey into Leonard Covello's classic memoir, *The Heart Is the Teacher* (1958). During his 45 years as a teacher and principal in the New York City Public Schools, Covello and a group of dedicated teachers, parents, and students created one of the first urban community schools concerned not only with academic programs but with the special needs of immigrant children. Covello's text has long been unavailable to the public. Perrone's discussion of Covello's experiences is a unique account of how one of today's most respected voices in educational reform has been touched and changed by an extraordinary reformer from the past.

Rose, Mike. (1989). *Lives on the Boundary: A Moving Account of the Struggles and Achievements of America's Educational Underclass.* New York: Penguin Books.

Mike Rose combines his own story with that of his students whose lives parallel his own. He describes his experiences and the methods he developed to introduce his unprepared students to the world of language and literature. He shows how he opens the doors that help them begin to reach their goals. A *Los Angeles Times* reviewer wrote: "*Lives on the Boundary* is a mirror to the many who may see their dreams translated into reality after all."

Tashlik, Phyllis. (1994. *Hispanic, Female and Young: An Anthology.* Houston: Pinata Books.

This volume captures the reality of what it means to be young, female, and Latina in New York City. The voices that speak through its pages are Las Mujeres Hispanas, a group of Latina teenagers at a public alternative school in El Barrio. The anthology incorporates the students' creative efforts and the literature that inspired them, combining the fresh perspectives of the younger women with those of seasoned, prize-winning authors. The resulting intergenerational dialogue includes remembrances of family and childhood, the difficulties and joys of growing up bilingual and bicultural, and what it is like to deal with both racism and misogynism. Most of all, it is a celebration of youth and of America's ethnic diversity.

The Freedom Writers. (1999). *The Freedom Writers Diary: How a Teacher and 150 Teens Used Writing to Change Themselves and the World Around Them.* New York: Main Street Books, Doubleday.

The subtitle says a lot! The book is composed of diary entries written over four years. It tells the story of a teacher and her diverse, "at-risk" students as they read, write, and learn together, particularly about the Holocaust with its implications about violence and tolerance intertwined with the writers' personal and developing lives. One reviewer, a prospective teacher, wrote: "I felt motivated and inspired by the metamorphosis of a first-year teacher, and her labeled and stereotyped students."

Walker, Kate. (2001). *Peter.* NewYork: Houghton Mifflin.

This is the story of Peter, a teenager who is coming to grips with the possibility that he might be gay. His experiences with individuals of the opposite sex and of his own sex lead him to believe that perhaps he is gay. The book deals with the pressures from peers and family and their reactions to the subject of gayness. (Although classified as fiction, the autobiographical nature of the story seems to warrant its inclusion in this list.)

Wasley, Patricia A. (1994). *Stirring the Chalkdust: Tales of Teachers Changing Classroom Practice.* New York Teachers College Press.

Patricia Wasley tells the stories of five secondary school teachers of different subjects who are in the midst of revising their practice to improve student performance. No longer satisfied with the compromises they've made for many years in high schools, these teachers are stirring their own most common practices to find better means to improved ends. The book provides a detailed, close-up view of teachers' daily lives and their work with colleagues, students, and parents, including images of classroom activity, planning sessions, and reflective interviews with teachers. This thoughtfully drawn portrait allows readers to understand what teachers are doing to make school a place where students learn to use their minds well.

Wood, G. W. (1998). *A Time to Learn: Creating Community in America's High Schools.* New York: Dutton.

This is the story of one high school's remarkable transformation and the people who made it happen. Wood offers guidelines, practical plans, and advice based on his observations and experiences at Federal Hocking High, as well as the results of his own trial and error. He focuses not on policy decisions or legislative debate but rather on the real lives of teachers and students. He shows how an understanding and appreciation of what goes on outside of school can have a positive effect on what happens in school. And he confronts the problems and social issues facing today's teenagers and presents viable solutions in which we, as responsible and caring citizens, can become the most effective instruments of change.

APPENDIX B

Teaching and Learning Hollywood Style

The following films are relevant to the subjects discussed in this text and are useful for sparking further discussion and debate.

Almost Famous (2000)
Anna and the King (1972)
Apt Pupil (1998)
Blackboard Jungle (1955)
Breakfast Club, The (1985)
Browning Version, The (1951, 1994)
Caterina Goes to the City (2005)
Center Stage (2000)
Children of a Lesser God (1986)
Class Act (1992)
Clueless (1995)
Coach Carter (2005)
Conrack (1997)
Corn Is Green, The (1945, 1979)
Dangerous Minds (1995),
Dead Poets Society (1989)
Educating Rita (1983)
Elephant (2003)
Emperor's Club, The (2002)
Etre et Avoir/To Be and to Have (2002)
Fast Times at Ridgemont High (1982)
Ferris Bueller's Day Off (9186)
Finding Forester (2000)
Goodbye Mr. Chips (1939, 1969)
Heaven Help Us (1985)
Hoop Dreams (1994)
Karate Kid, The (1984)
Kindergarten Cop (1990)
Lean on Me (1989)
Mad Hot Ballroom (2005
Man Without a Face, The ((1993)
Mean Girls (2004))
Miracle Worker, The (1962)
Mona Lisa Smile (2003)
Mr. Holland's Opus (1996)
Music of the Heart (1999)
My Fair Lady (1964)
Napoleon Dynamite (2005)
October Sky (1999)
Our Miss Brooks (1956)

Paper Chase, The (1973)

Prime of Miss Jean Brodie, The (1969)

Pump Up the Volume (1990)

Pygmalion (1938)

Remember the Titans (2000)

Renaissance Man (1994)

Rushmore (1999)

Searching for Bobby Fisher (1993)

School of Rock (2003)

Sisterhood of the Traveling Pants (2005)

Sounder (1972)

Stand and Deliver (1988)

Teachers (1984)

To Sir with Love (1967)

Up the Down Staircase (1967)

With Honors (1994)

INDEX